IS ANYTHING ALRIGHT?

IS ANYTHING ALRIGHT?

MY TITANICS STORY

Stanley N Hyman

Published in 2014 by:

Stellar Books LLP
Dunham Gatehouse
Charcoal Road
Bowdon
Cheshire
WA14 4RY
UK

w: www.stellarbooks.co.uk
e: info@stellarbooks.co.uk

Typeset by Stellar Books LLP
Edited by Patricia C Byron

ISBN: 978-1910275016

A copy of this book is available in the British Library

*Dedicated to my children, grandchildren
and any future generations.
Not forgetting all my amazing staff
and customers who made the writing
of this book possible.*

CONTENTS

ACKNOWLEDGEMENTS

My story has been written down for the benefit of all the grandchildren and any future generations. At present time we have Eliana, Callum, Jack, Ruby, Leo, Talia, Jessica, Ronnie and Billy.

They will be able to read and, hopefully, be amused recalling some of the situations and exploits that happened to me, Grandpa Stan, during my tenure of the JA Hyman (Titanics) dynasty for nearly fifty years. It has been a labour of love recalling some of the yarns of yesteryear although I have had to change some of the names in these stories to protect the guilty!

Having an attention span of the proverbial hamster and usually moving on to another interest every few months I find that writing this has been for me an unusual achievement and has taxed me to the limit of my powers of concentration and self-discipline.

All this would not have been possible without having had the privilege of looking after my wonderful customers whom I hope thought as much about me as

I thought about them. We had great relationships. Sharing with each other the sad occasions as well as the happy ones.

Writing this story has brought back to me all the fun times I have been through over the years. The customers were my friends and I now realise that we all looked after each other. It was always a two way relationship.

I was I must confess, to all intents, a bigamist; being married and looking after two families. My wife and children during the evenings and part of the weekends and my customers during the daytime. No wonder I was always exhausted.

Now I must record my eternal thanks to my Jen, my life companion. I remember walking down the aisle looking adoringly at my beautiful, young bride, I inadvertently trod on the train of her wedding dress. Seconds after being married she gave me THE LOOK and I have never forgotten it some forty-nine years later.

Jennifer, née Barsh, has always been my rock and inspiration. She has been my sounding board and advisor. Our partnership has been always a shared one. She has been and still is a wonderful mum to her children and has never been shy in giving her forthright opinions, whether asked for or not. She has been instrumental in the children's education through kindergarten and North Cheshire Jewish Primary School and then, to her great joy, all three of our children Danielle, Richard and Emma passed the examination for Cheadle Hulme School, where she herself was educated. The children then fulfilled her dreams by all going to university and all three acquiring degrees.

Jennifer herself, while bringing up the children, started studying again and gained her own degree as a mature student. No mean feat, whilst juggling with all the needs of her young family.

My Jennifer was and is still, thankfully, my mentor and confidante. A loyal and beautiful lady, without whose help and encouragement I would not have succeeded in writing this story. We have had a unique relationship and may we continue to annoy and exasperate each other for many years to come.

I would like to thank Michael Rich, our first next door neighbour in Delamere Road, Gatley after we were married. He was my dentist until he escaped many years ago to the Deep South to become a gamekeeper and no longer a poacher. Known to all the children as Uncle Grumpy. The help and encouragement he has given me has been invaluable in the writing of this book.

My grateful thanks to Elaine Lewis. Without her technical skill of downloading memory sticks and all sorts of magical computer wizardry I would still be writing with a quill and ink.

Thanks also to Philip Weisberg for suggesting the apt title of this book.

I must also thank our religious leaders, who have made many interesting decisions during my working life. Without their moral help and support there would not be a vibrant, kosher Manchester. They are a modern and tolerant organisation and are essential to ensure the continuity of our faith and they deserve the full support of our community.

My thanks finally to all the goodies, baddies and the interesting characters that dipped in and out of my life for their contributions which have made this story possible. Also my apologies to anyone I may have forgotten or offended.

INTRODUCTION

Grandpa Joseph Abraham Hyman started his incredible voyage through life in 1880 in the deepest recesses of mother Russia. Realising that there was little future for Jews in this vast continent, other than being the servants and playthings of vodka swilling natives and blood thirsty Cossacks, he decided, with thousands of other citizens, to emigrate whilst able.

He had a cousin who had offered him shelter and accommodation in Glasgow where he settled and lived until the call of the big city and a young lady, one Esther Levy - the daughter of Chaim Yankel, a milkman, lured him to the great metropolis of Manchester. No one is sure if he had understood quite what was offered along with young Esther, whether it was a dairy or a dowry as he still spoke in broken biscuits.; this being Scottish English, with a Russian accent.

They duly married and moved into accommodation in Lord Street, Cheetham, along with their very small herd of livestock, which consisted of one cow that existed in the back yard and began manufacturing smetna and kess which, loosely translated, is sour cream and cream cheese, which they sold to the locals to eke out a meagre existence. There they lived and thrived, producing five children in quick succession. No tele in those days!

Grandpa in the meantime had been in contact with a relative who lived in Philadelphia in the USA, who kept asking him to visit and realise the potential it afforded. He should come and discover this amazing land full of opportunity and start a new and meaningful life for his family and himself.

Grandpa realised that opportunities to improve his future in England at that time were few and far between. His American cousin promised that he would be their sponsor. He managed to convince Esther that a trip to America was needed, where he could go and find a new and exciting life for them. This could and would only happen once. What could he lose by visiting, and see the wonderful potential it could offer? After all the streets in America were paved with gold. It was now or never. WHAT COULD POSSIBLY GO WRONG?

Was it a coincidence or was it fate? Nobody will ever know. There was a super liner, the largest ever built full of modern technology, guaranteed unsinkable, that was sailing on her maiden voyage to New York in the April of 1912. What an adventure!

Not only to go to New York but to sail on this new super liner called *Titanic*! Everyone knows what happened next.

Joseph had been travelling steerage and had been fortunate enough to be on the deck that night marvelling at the magnificent sight of the majestic, huge icebergs, glistening in the bright moonlight as they floated past on this clear and starry night. He was watching as if hypnotised by these strange phenomena when the ship collided with one, virtually the same size and height as the *Titanic*. He did not think too much about this incident, and continued to watch this surreal and amazing spectacle. Feeling in his pocket for his hip flask full of brandy, there in case it became very cold. Little did he realise that this drop of brandy would some few hours later help to save his life. As the night wore on it became apparent that something awful was happening and the boat was sinking.

As he was travelling steerage and was lucky enough to be on deck he was asked if he would row a lifeboat as the first and second class passengers could nor would not demean themselves and indulge in manual labour. The rest is tragic history. He was rescued by the *Carpathia* and some days later landed in New York.

He spent several months there with relatives during which time he saw the new and interesting foods in

Third-Class Passengers—British/Southampton Embarkment

Abbott, Eugene	Davies, Alfred	Goodwin, Sidney (child)
Abbott, Rosa	Davies, John	Green, George
Abbott, Rossmore	Davies, Joseph	Guest, Robert
Abbing, Anthony	Davison, Thomas H.	Harknett, Alice
Adams, J.	*Davison, Mary*	Harmer, Abraham
Aks, Filly	Dean, Mr. Bertram F.	*Hee, Ling*
Aks, Leah	*Dean, Mrs. Hetty*	*Howard, May*
Alexander, William	*Dean, Bertran (child)*	*Hyman, Abraham*
Allen, William	*Dean, Vera (infant)*	Johnston, A. G.
Allum, Owen G.	Dennis, Samuel	Johnston, Mrs.
Badman, Emily	Dennis, William	Johnston, William (child)
Barton David	Derkings, Edward	Johnston, Mrs. C. H. (child)
Beavan, W. T.	*Derkings, Elizabeth*	Johnson, Mr. A.
Billiard, A. van	*Dowdell, Elizabeth*	Johnson, Mr. W.
Billiard, James (child)	*Drapkin, Jenie*	Keefe, Arthur
Billiard, Walter (child)	*Dugemin, Joseph*	Kelly, James
Bing, Lee	*Elsbury, James*	*Lam, Ali*
Bowen, David	*Emanuel, Ethel (child)*	Lam, Len
Braund, Lewis	Everett, Thomas J.	*Lang, Fang*
Braund, Owen	Ford, Arthur	Leonard, Mr. L
Brocklebank, William	Ford, Margaret	Lester, J.
Cann, Erenst	Ford, Mrs. D. M.	*Ling, Lee*
Carver, A.	Ford, Mr. E. W.	Lithman, Simon
Celotti, Francesco	Ford, M. W. T. N.	Lobb, Cordelia
Chip, Chang	Ford, Maggie (child)	Lobb, William A.
Christmann, Emil	Franklin, Charles	Lockyer, Edward
	Garthfirth, John	*Lovell, John*
		MacKay, George W.

Part of the Passenger list from the Titanic.
The names of survivors are in italics.

the New York delis: salamis, salt beef and smoked salmon to name a few. This gave him the idea of opening a delicatessen store in Manchester on his return. The problem was that he was terrified of sailing on a boat; he couldn't pluck up courage to go home and join up with his wife and family. Unfortunately there was no other way of returning to England. One night his friends managed to get him drunk and before he had sobered up, he was on a ship already sailing back home.

When he arrived back in the UK he set about opening a delicatessen store based on what he had seen in New York. The family moved out of Lord Street to a new up and coming Jewish area at 230 Waterloo Road.

The name of the business would become obvious, as each and every time he walked up or down the road people would nudge each other and say in awe:

'Look! There's the man from the *Titanic*!'

And that, quite simply, is how we acquired our name.

Grandpa Joseph Abraham Hyman with his first wife Esther.

★

Some nine months after Grandpa Joseph returned from his ill-fated trip, my father was born.... Grandpa could never be accused of wasting time. They named him Harry Jonas. The second name after the biblical story of the miracle of Jonah and the Whale, Jonah having been saved from a watery grave by a miracle with this whale ….As was Grandpa from the *Titanic*.

The family of seven thrived for a time until alas, as in a lot of families, siblings fell out especially after marriage when in laws became involved.

My father had served in India for four years during the Second World War and on his return the infighting had become so intense that the business had to be divided. Because dad had been in the RAF he was granted a special licence which gave him privileges to produce certain products. When the shit really hit the fan he swapped his manufacturing licence and the factory in Percival Street the family was running, for the shop premises at 230/2 Waterloo Road.

I started work as a Sunday boy helping out in 1954 at the age of thirteen and started work officially at the age of sixteen and was not encouraged to finish my formal education at Stand Grammar School. I suppose that I received my degree at the university of life.

Enough! Now let's get on with the stories!

J A Hyman Ltd, Titanics.

CHAPTER 1

All The World's a Stage, and I...

One moment in time is what it was and what it seemed like. When man once again thought he could outsmart and overcome Mother Nature; it was sheer arrogance and, tragically, very stupid. The tragedy that fateful day in April 1912 had an upside. Every down has an up in life. The one positive thing was the creation of a dynasty which, one hundred years on, is still going strong and is now in the capable hands of my son Richard. You must understand you don't actually own Titanics but are the guardian of a legacy handed down from father to son.

I was that guardian from the early 1970s until 2000 and something. I was actively involved for fifty years or so, but Grandpa Hyman didn't leave me much when he passed away in 1954 when I was thirteen. Or did he? The mystique of Titanics has a fascination that has grown with time and is very much a part of Manchester folklore. For me, it is a story akin to the likes of Robin Hood.

There are many incidents that can happen in a span of fifty years; too many to remember all but there were many great friends and mentors who kept me strong when there were bad days. There were many difficult days: compulsory purchase of the spiritual home at No. 230-232 Waterloo Road and, when we moved, the very council which evicted us paid out the proverbial peanuts. It was legal robbery but that's another story.

It was the goodness and the understanding of the late Sydney Friedland, my banker for some three decades, who saved the day, the years and the on-going legacy and I have always been grateful. When Dad had his heart attack in the office in front of me I realised that all of a sudden the buck stopped with me and our survival depended on my wits and leadership. It was very scary knowing that your wife, three children and all our staff now relied on me to provide. Luckily I had four great guys who helped me in those early days: in the names of my Dad, Jack Barsh, Louis Grenard and Jack Firestone.

Dad was a very gentle man, who excelled in many interesting pastimes and sports. He was a pilot way back in 1936, a master bowman in archery, captain of the Manchester Fencing team, an excellent golfer and, latterly, a prize winning fisherman. Life must have been very tough for him and my Mum after the tragic death of my younger brother David but they put on a very brave face for the outside world and continued to live with much courage and dignity. He taught me the tenets for correct behaviour in life and I felt proud to be able to continue and further the business by his example.

January 1945. Harry Hyman in uniform - My Dad.

Jack Barsh, my father in law, was for many years the President of the Jewish Communal Council. He was a fine upright man who, in my opinion, gave more to the council than to his own business. He was a great community man who could, very eloquently, stand his corner in any discussion or debate. Although a passionate

Manchester City supporter, he never went to any of the games but he still gave his opinion and analysis. I remember one match day when I did not know, or want to know, the final score. If my memory serves me the match was against Spurs. Jen and I had been out and I was going to watch the highlights on Match of the Day. Sky Sports had not been invented yet. Excitement mounting, I begged him not to tell me the score. He promised he would not but told me that they had been so unlucky. Thanks Jack! They had lost 1-2 in the last minute.

Being slightly flippant, Jack enjoyed a good funeral. I seem to recall his best day was one Sunday when he helped officiate at two unveilings and a funeral, all on the same afternoon. (Grave stone unveilings, for those who don't know, take place once the grave stone is erected, which can take place up to eleven months after a death and is usually attended by the family and friends.) He had a lovely voice and was more than able to conduct all the prayers, melodiously and with dignity. It kept him animated for weeks.

Louis Grenard, was a clapper by trade. Now for the uninformed, a clapper was a person who knocked on the doors of mostly the gentry, or anyone they knew who had had a recent bereavement. He would offer his condolences and ask, in a very posh and polite voice, if there were any artefacts that they wished to dispose of.

Louis was born in Portsmouth, the youngest of 14. His father was a ships chandler and I presume he came to Manchester to make a living. Being the youngest of the family he must have had to fight for his corner in life. He was not everyone's favourite as he was pretty ruthless. His methods of extracting goods from grieving widows must have permeated down to his private life and he was not always popular with his peers. Louis had taken a shine to me and he would take me out clapping. He had an amazing skill and could scan a room in fewer than ten seconds and evaluate if there was anything worth buying.

I remember one incident when we called at a house and the poor lady, whose husband had presumably only just passed away, showed Louis her late husband's gold watch. Although it brought back fond memories and was of great sentimental value she desperately needed the money to pay for his funeral. Louis was, apparently, full of concern for this poor lady's plight and, wiping away a crocodile tear, he purchased the watch. He then took from his pocket a small jeweller's hammer and smashed the watch. He then proceeded to give all the bits back to the lady to remind her of her husband and he took the gold case. All heart! I was as gob-smacked as this poor lady. We beat a hasty retreat.

Louis went off to Hanging Ditch in Manchester, where all the dealers hung out, to sell his daily purchases and then went straight to the bookies to blow in his profit. He would, though, give me great advice and taught me that if you really wanted to succeed in life, you had to work hard and, as everyone has opportunities in life and business, to grasp them when they occur and never let them slip through your fingers. I often asked how I would know and he always said that when they happened I would know. He was right. Maybe it was not all luck.

Jack Firestone, who had been a kosher poultry dealer, had been partners with my uncle, Gerry Marcus. They had a chicken slaughter house in Howard Street at the bottom of Waterloo Road. Jack was a very gentle and kind man who had to put up with all the carryings on of his partner, my Uncle Gerry. Gerry was a great practical joker and how Jack stood for all the nonsense was unbelievable.

One such incident occurred when the Alfred Hitchcock film 'The Birds' was being screened at the Premier cinema in Cheetham Hill Road. Uncle Gerry armed with a live chicken went to see the film, sat himself on the front row of the balcony and when the scary scene in the film where the birds attacked the humans came on, threw this live chicken over the balcony and created panic and mayhem in the cinema. Crazy, but if you weren't in the cinema that night it was very funny. Jack had to pay his fine.

These guys had all retired and used to assemble Monday to Thursday in the office and put the world to rights. Smoked salmon sandwiches, drinks and I had my Dad and the three wise men to ask advice. This was wonderful for me as they were able to impart their experiences and wisdom. They were a great help to me when I had a problem, big or small. I realise that it was beneficial for them too, giving them a focal point and demonstrating that they were still useful members of society. It proved to me that there is no substitute for experience, especially when they are on your side. We have many adversaries in business and you need all the help you can get. I was very lucky having the advice and support of these guys. They had sound understanding and common sense, a trait that only comes with years of experience. I thank them all for their company and their sense of humour.

My role in J.A.Hyman (Titanics), 'The Shop' or 'JAH', was clearly defined: I was responsible for everything. This was self-inflicted, as my delegation skills were nil. This put a great pressure on my family but my stoic and very capable wife Jen ran the house, family and me with apparent ease, thus enabling me to be single minded providing a living for us all.

I look back and try to rationalise what made it work and I believe one of the reasons was that we at JAH and the customers looked after each other. We, on our part, tried to help the community and although we were in business for profit, we offered a sort of two way community service. We supported them the best way we could by being very fair with our prices, personal service and support to the less fortunate.

Every day a presentation was staged, as if we were in a production, me being the leading actor who chatted up all who came to see this daily performance. Most seemed to like the risqué, funny show and the customers enjoyed being the audience. People like to be noticed, to be made a fuss of and to feel important because they are.

CHAPTER 2

Sunday Mornings

S unday morning was the highlight of the week, not just for us but for all the ethnic shops in Manchester. We had to have a licence and sign a declaration that acknowledged the Sabbath, as one was only allowed to open for six days in a week.

Of course being a Jewish shop, Saturday, in the winter at least, was for resting, praying and football matches. Sunday morning was a morning of analysis as to why City were always unlucky and the arch enemy United were always jammy and ground out fluky results, the conclusion being that the Almighty is a red so what chance did we have? This was the considered opinions of the greatest experts of their time, namely the Marcus family, my Mum's brothers.

Sunday was when all the men folk would drive down to Waterloo Road to discuss these important issues of the time and to find out how unlucky they had been with that treble. If only the favourite had come in first instead of third in the second race they would have won a monkey (£500). Instead, it was *gornisht,* unlucky except for the bookies. This was the general chat for a regular Sunday.

Uncle Nat, donning white apron, would bring out with great ceremony the wooden cutting board, sharpen a large carving knife on a steel and then, and only then, would immerse a huge fork into a large container of boiling water and out would emerge a great big pickled brisket with a wonderful covering of fat and the delightful aroma of hot pickle and garlic. A large black bread was sliced and the gathered assembly would surge forward to try the first hot brisket sandwich of the day….

'Plenty of mustard and don't tell my Missus but put plenty of fat on too and don't forget the pickled sweet and sour cucumber.'

Everyone contentedly munching would then buy their smoked salmon at 7/6d per quarter (37p per 120 gram). Fussnogge, hot dogs, two kinds being sold at five shillings a pound on a silver tray and the better quality ones (for the more discerning punter) sold on a gold tray at 7/6d a pound and what a different quality they were… so I was told by my Dad. And who was I to argue? At one thirty all the customers would go home happy and back to their diets and we would cash up and go home for a well-earned rest.

CHAPTER 3

The Bank

It's funny how the world and things have evolved for the better, or is it for the worse? One such episode I recall in my younger days happened every Friday.

Our shop in Waterloo Road was next door to Martins Bank (now Barclays). In those days a bank was a respected institution, a veritable pillar in the community that helped and integrated local people and businesses in the area. Our local manager was Mr L; he was a great friend to the local businessmen who would go in to him for a loan or financial help. Now it was well known that the best way to obtain this help was to go armed with a bottle of gin, set it on the table, and put your case forward. Three tumblers later the help was forthcoming. The fascinating fact from all these meetings, as far as I am aware, was that no one ever let him down. The gin was like WD40, it just oiled the cogs of commerce and made Mr L happy and glowing and benevolent.

Every Friday we had to get change for our busy Sunday morning and, week in and week out, Dad always forgot until 3.00pm when the bank was closing. My job was to go to the bank and bring back £5 of pennies, three penny bits, sixpences, shillings and half crowns. We never used 'florins' as they were called, they were two shilling pieces. The problem was that the bank closed at 3.00pm and was, therefore, officially closed. I always knocked on the closed doors and was let in by the very pretty cashier, Kathy, who gave me 'The Look' as all women do, and would tell me, as they were busy cashing up, to go and help myself as I knew where everything was. I can't imagine that happening today.

All the bank staff became good friends and Graham, one of the loyal staff, later joined Round Table with me and Kathy, the Ladies Circle. They are still in touch with Jen and me after fifty years and it still seems like yesterday.

Another episode with our lovely Martins Bank was when they installed their very first alarm system. This consisted of a buzzer being installed in our shop as we were next door; if and when this buzzer went off, we were supposed to call the police. The problem was that this alarm seemed to have a life of its own and went off with monotonous regularity.

I remember one fine spring morning the alarm buzzing and one of our brighter employees, Lilly, if my memory serves me correctly, ambled into the bank and asked the bank staff if this was a bank job or just another false alarm. Thankfully this was the latter and Lilly lived to serve another day.

CHAPTER 4

Crossing the Great Divide

My children often asked why Jean and Harry Hyman, along with their two sons, David and me, crossed the great north south divide and decided to settle in the calmer waters of Didsbury.

Way back in the 1950s the Beth Din was, and still is, the governing body who oversaw the total kosher meat trade in Manchester. They had the power to open, to close, to fine or suspend any butcher who, in their view, had transgressed the sacred and sanctified laws of kashrus. The power behind the throne, whose grand title of Clerk to the Court, was a gentleman called the Reverend Sigmund Margolies. Known irreverently as Ziggy, but not to his face.

Now I am not stating that all the butchers were angels at that particular time, but he scared the shit out of them. He would fine or suspend anyone who had committed an offence appertaining to Judaism or the laws relating to the selling of kosher meat or poultry, as he maintained that the kosher butcher should be of the highest moral and religious beliefs. They were, after all, the main custodians and trustees of the housewife's kosher kitchen.

There was a wide spectrum of misdemeanours. The most heinous being the selling of *treife,* non-kosher meat or poultry and the least serious, in my view only, was to be seen in a car on a Saturday afternoon, Saturday being the holiest day of the week, going presumably to follow their dreams at City or United. Those were the days when it was synagogue in the morning and a football match in the afternoon.

I remember as a child seeing my Dad entering by the rear door of a friend's car and watching in amazement as he covered himself over with a blanket provided for him so he would not be recognised and lying completely still like an absconding fugitive until the car was out of the neighbourhood and wending its way to Old Trafford. It must have been an interesting sight for curious onlookers seeing prone bodies covered by blankets being transported in the backs of cars on a Saturday afternoon and suddenly stirring themselves and sitting up when they were out of the danger zone.

The Reverend Sigmund also placed, in strategic nooks, crannies and corners, Beth Din spies, suitably disguised with long beards and big black hats, so that they would blend as naturally as possible into the local streets of Higher Crumpsall and Prestwich. These guys were zealously doing their job and looked on it as a messianic calling to shop some poor butcher or delicatessen owner for transgressing the holy day. Besides they were paid well for their information. These gentlemen were all part of the Reverend Sigmund's network and, as he put it, that if the Manchester Jewish butchers did not fear their Lord enough then he would give them something else to fear. And he succeeded.

Every town throughout the country that had a Jewish community had their own Beth Din and Shechita board governing them. The boundaries for selling were clearly defined by the governing authorities. Butcher shops could only sell raw meat or poultry and grocery/delicatessen shops were only allowed to buy any cooked meats made by a local manufacturer. Each organisation ran independently, and was fiercely protected, as it was an excellent source of income for them. We were not allowed to buy or sell any raw or cooked meat and poultry from any other town, thus preserving the dictatorial and autocratic status of the local Jewish authorities.

Woe betide anyone who tried to purchase any of the aforementioned goods, raw meat or poultry from some out of town authority. They would be summoned to the board, have the swinging light treatment and at the very least - be fined, suspended or even have their licence revoked. Then there would be the public humiliation of seeing their name and misdemeanour in the Jewish Gazette or Telegraph telling the local community that the shop was no longer part of the Manchester Beth Din and was closed down and that was that. It was the metaphorical public hanging and the readers of the aforementioned journals were the tricoteuses; they loved the scandal and the ensuing gossip it provoked.

It made it difficult as a young person at that particular time to understand all of this and now some fifty years on I still cannot work them out. Was, for instance, the kosher meat in London not kosher? Of course it was. I could only presume that the lowest common denominator in our religion or, I suppose anybody else's, was not entirely being a god-fearing person and supporting the good Lord but power and money but, alas, mainly money. I maintain that some people are losing the plot and are worshipping their religion and not God.

As the authorities had the absolute monopoly for kosher products and the good people of Manchester were only allowed to buy their kosher foods from local shops, this gave them a literal and metaphorical cash cow. They reasoned that the supervision fees generated from the local kosher stores would supply them with an easy income for ever and there was no need to even think of diversifying and finding other means of supplementing their funds. How wrong they were.

At this particular time my parents had the opportunity of opening a grocery shop in Lapwing Lane in Didsbury, which had been owned and run by the Samuels family. There was also Bookbinders bread shop along with Kregers, the kosher butcher next door. It seemed a logical and good idea to have an excuse to be able to escape from the claustrophobic clutches of the north Manchester mafia, spies and all. There was already a large community of Jews in south Manchester but the majority were different from us northerners as they were disrespectfully referred to as Yakipaks, Sephardic Jews from Spanish and Portuguese origins. They mostly lived in West Didsbury and were rudely known as the Jews of Palestine Road, which was really Palatine Road.

The shop flourished and as my Mum had the task of running the store, it was decided to take the plunge and move the family from Rothesay Road in Crumpsall to the leafy suburbs of Didsbury, in the south, and escape from the suffocating confines of the north. Thus crossing the great divide. The defining line between North and South being the River Irwell, which did not part for us so we used a bridge. The same bridge that had daubed on it for many years 'Save the Rosenbergs', who they were no one was quite sure. It was rumoured that they had been Communist spies and were executed by the Americans in the era of the cold war, good old McCarthyism. But this Victoria Bridge was the main crossing from north to south, especially if one lived in the Cheetham Hill area of Manchester.

Now as the world evolved, changes started in peoples' eating habits across the country and even the kosher food world. Slowly at first and then gathering momentum, people had started travelling and tasting and enjoying new and exciting foods that they had discovered whilst on holiday.

Israel became a large exporter of cooked meats to the UK and they were distributed to the Jewish wholesalers for them to distribute to the local shops and stores. This created a major problem, especially for us, as we were not allowed to sell these goods as the local Beth Din did not approve. There were two main reasons; the first being that they said that the kashrut was not up to their standards so the butchers and delicatessens under their jurisdiction would not be allowed to sell them. But the second and, I personally felt, that the main reason was that they were not initially consulted and would not be getting a share.

The two local wholesalers, Messrs Goldstein and Rosenthal started distributing these Israeli chicken and turkey products to non-approved that is to non-Beth Din grocery shops and we as a delicatessen shop were finding it difficult to compete as we were only allowed to sell the products that we had traditionally sold for generations. Rather than just put our head in the sand and gently fade away it was decided to became pro-active.

We started selling raw meat. The good butchers of Manchester and districts were not very pleased with this new competition and there were many complaints to the religious authorities. I was summoned the BD headquarters on Cheetham Hill Road and asked to explain. I took a deep breath and decided to stand my ground and told them that if they stopped the local wholesaler from distributing foreign meat products then we would happily go back to the status quo. I was told that they could or would not try to do anything about it but their licensees would not be able to sell these products. I suggested that instead of the housewife koshering the meat at home, as they had always traditionally done by soaking in water for thirty minutes, then salting the meat for one hour and then to finish off this tedious, laborious and very necessary process, dipping it twice into running cold water. This made kosher meat koshered and we would be the first to do it for them.

After a long debate they decided that we would be allowed to sell raw meat and poultry but only pre packed in a frozen state. Nothing was ever straightforward. If the meat was to be sold frozen then it would of course have to be koshered first. Up to this time butchers would sell the kosher meat to the good ladies of Manchester, then they would have to the take it home and kosher it in water and salt.

From those early beginnings every kosher butcher in the country now sell only koshered meat and poultry and I wager that instead of every Jewish housewife being able to kosher their meat in the 1950s none in the 21st century would have the remotest idea how to do this arduous task now. Well done to us; I never thought of myself being a revolutionary.

A few years later we opened two butchers' shops in south Manchester. The first in Cheadle in the 1970s with my uncle Nat and latterly the second in Hale /Altrincham and the legacy is still carrying on in the capable hands of my son Richard.

CHAPTER 5

The Good Lord Works in Strangeways

Looking back, my working life seemed to be Passover orientated. Life seemed to be determined by the craziness of that period of the year. In fact, if I could have had my way, the JAH calendar year would have run from April to March, the latter part of April being the dawning and the light and March usually being the dark and the bleakest time, despite the 28th being my birthday.

I can only ponder and think that if my Dad had just kept himself to himself and had kept his powder dry for another month his first son Stanley would have been able to enjoy a birthday instead of the sheer dread of working through this annual crackers exodus. After all, the children of Israel only had to endure forty years of wandering and I've had to put up with fifty. But as the late Joe Rubins of Mrs. Elswood fame always told me: 'Passover might mean matzos to the customers but it was bread and butter for you'.

One of my earliest recollections of Passover, was when I was just eighteen years of age. One of my jobs was to deliver the Passover foods in the Morris Minor shooting-brake directly to Strangeways prison. We Jews have always had our fair share of wrongdoers and there were always a few prisoners who were being entertained by Her Majesty every year. On an average, so I was told, usually about four or five but the prison officers had told me that on the lead up to this festival the Jewish ranks seemed to double and on some years even treble or more. They told me that the fervour to be one of the faith was nothing to do with matzos or even the excitement of eating prunes. Not even the Seder Night and reciting the four questions, but simply that the Jewish prisoners on that night drank four cups of wine. Wine was alcohol and this was definitely a no-no in HMP Strangeways. So when the festival was approaching, the Passover order for our true brothers and the more recent converts was quite substantial.

The delivery was always exciting, if a little scary, especially for a young lad being able to drive to and deliver goods into the bowels and inner sanctum of this appalling Victorian jail. I would collect The Very Reverend Doctor Slotkie from his house in Bignor Street and drive to the main entrance, which was situated in Sherbourne Street. Doctor Slotkie would present our credentials to the gate man and the huge intimidating solid oak Victorian doors would creak and swing open onto a dark and forbidding courtyard.

We were given an escort and I had to reverse the van about a hundred yards down a narrow alley with dark satanic walls all around us. Shadowy shapes of prisoners behind barred cell windows shouted obscenities at us and we were even asked if we had secreted any files inside the sticks of salami. Not the most pleasant place to be.

The prison Chaplain would take charge of the goods as they had to be kept separately from the normal everyday food which, of course, was *chometz,* as well of not being quite kosher and definitely not to be used for Passover. The senior warden would ceremoniously commandeer the wine, which would be kept safely locked in the Governor's office until its use on the Seder Night. Everything being signed for, we would drive and edge slowly out of the alleyway to the main gates and, thankfully, back to freedom and liberty.

I reckon if more people could have seen what it was like in this prison there would be, or should have been, far fewer miscreants as it was very scary and intimidating. Haven't times changed? I do not think that some 50 years on one would be able to drive a van in and out of a prison. Nowadays it's probably easier to get out than to go in.

Some years later, in April 1990, the sun was beating down which was most unusual for that time of the year, especially in Manchester. Just as another Passover scrum was nicely getting underway one of the locals ran into the shop shouting:

'Stan!! It's happening! In't it great?'

'What could be great at this time of the year?' I asked him.

'They are rioting!' came the reply.

'Who are they?' I asked, wondering if the long suffering City supporters had finally had enough and decided to riot…

'No! The prisoners at Strangeways are on the roof and are throwing slates at the warders down below!' was the reply.

Sure enough one could see the top of the prison bedecked with bright apparel and some prisoners standing precariously on the roof waving banners and wrenching off bits of roof as ammunition ready to hurl at the officers below. What a surreal sight. It was as if you were on something and having a very odd dream. Maybe Pesach was finally getting to me. But no, it was real enough.

On the following morning the sun was still shining as brightly as the previous day, a beautiful day for a riot. We were greeted not only with the rush of early Passover shoppers, but with vans full of TV news crews. The media interest created by the prison uprising was going international. This was great for us for two reasons, the first being that the news crews were out most of the day looking for food as watching a riot from a safe distance makes you hungry and it made for the first time a very eventful Passover. It was the first and only time that it was exciting to be in work early at this particular time of the year.

The riot lasted for a week and finally ended just as the Passover was beginning. A great talking point and there were a lot more than four questions from the children on that particular year.

Inside 1950s Titanics and my Dad serving behind the counter.
Copyright Lynn Millard The Grocers Gazette.

CHAPTER 6

Fur, Fish and Feathers

The instructions were very simple: firstly feed the cat, then the fish and finally the budgies. When these chores were completed, prepare the shop for the customers.

My parents had gone away on a short holiday for a well-earned break and, for the first time in my life, I was sort of in charge. Being in my late teens at the time, my mind was not focused solely on work but on the far loftier thoughts that concerned an eighteen year old.

In the mid-twentieth century the hygiene laws were so different. They were far more lenient than they are today and it was not unusual to have a cat on the premises, primarily as a pet but also for the security of the building and its contents at night time.

Our cat was my Dad's favourite. It could do no wrong. The staff believed that it was a spy disguised as a cat and would report to Dad any misdemeanours that had happened when he was not around.

It would wait for him at the door every morning, not moving until he arrived. On seeing Dad it would suddenly spring into life purring as loud as it could. 'That F***ing Cat' as it was called, as it had not been given a proper name, would follow him to his office and once Dad had taken his jacket off and sat down, would then sit on his shoulders wrapping itself round him like a scarf and looking disapprovingly at anyone or anything that had cause to interrupt this unusual union. When Dad had to move, the cat would reluctantly undrape itself and sit curled up on his chair, waiting for his return.

As a feline, it had unusual and weird tastes, its favourite snack being black olives. In the 1950s olives, Polish sour cucumbers and herrings were packed in large wooden barrels. These barrels were opened up and every morning large plastic trays were filled from them for display purposes. Each night the contents of the trays would be deposited back in the barrels and the trays would be washed ready for the next day. This cat, when the fancy took it, would climb on to the edge of the olive barrel and delicately dangle a paw into the depths as though it was fishing until it was able to retrieve an olive.

When he had scooped up his treat the cat would retreat back to the office, nibbling away at his snack leaving the discarded olive stone on the desk as if it were his trophy that he had donated to my Dad. This caused quite a lot of excitement with children, who insisted that their parents took them shopping with them to see Harry's performing cat. As a reward for shopping with their parents and seeing this unbelievable but truly amazing cat acrobat, my Dad would give every child who came into the store a Jewish lollypop. A Jewish lolly, for those who don't know, is the wing cut from the side of a smoked salmon. It was (and still is) the best tasting and most succulent part of the fish. Dad would wrap the wing up in a piece of greaseproof paper, with part sticking out, and the kids would nibble at the salmon like eating a lolly, hence the name.

Our goldfish lived in three tanks that took up the entire length of the internal windows of the shop. Dad had told all the children who visited the premises that they were miniature salmon and he was waiting for them to grow and when they were big enough he would be able to smoke them.

They never seemed to do much except what fish normally do, that is go round and round in circles. A detailed head and tail count revealed that at one of Dad's censuses we had approximately fifty fish in each tank.

They certainly were a local attraction, people would often stop just to watch these fish in large tanks as it was quite a rare sight to see aquariums in those days, especially in Hightown.

As the weeks went by there seemed to be a problem with the numbers of Dad's fish family, as their numbers appeared to be declining. After a count, it was discovered that there were only about forty in each tank. Something fishy was going on. The mystery was eventually solved by a passer-by, who told us what was happening. It had caused a great deal of amusement with the locals when at night Dad's favourite black cat would sit at the side of the fish tank, and when the mood or fancy took him he would dangle a paw into the tank and scoop up a little extra supper for himself, much to the amusement of his audience who applauded every time he landed a fish. I don't think that the cat ever forgave us for stopping his nightly snack when we started covering the fish tanks at night.

The cat did eventually get its comeuppance and meet its maker when, one cold and wintry day, it was run over by a customer's car.

★

The fashionable pets of the time were budgies, every child had at least one. The birdcage would always be in the living room and all the birds seemed to be called Joey. We were no exception, except that we housed hundreds in our shop at number 230 Waterloo Road.

Our budgies lived in a huge cage somewhere in the depths of the building, about ten feet off the floor on top of an old commercial refrigerator. I am not quite sure how my Dad became a bird man, but he did have many strange hobbies. Maybe he had been influenced by the late Percy Edwards, animal impersonator and ornithologist. I was not sure but he became a very successful budgie breeder. I think that it was more by luck than skill. I knew that there were more than one hundred from the amount of Trill, the popular budgie food of this era, which was purchased and consumed. Every week or so more budgies would hatch out. This could have caused an acute overcrowding problem, which was overcome by giving away as many as possible. I remember a notice displayed in the shop stating something like 'Bring your own cage, it's all the rage and takeaway a blue or yellow budgerigar for free'. Not a bad marketing ploy.

As I mentioned earlier Mum and Dad were away and this pretty little girl, carrying a bird cage, was brought in by her Mum to buy their shopping for the weekend. Her Mum had seen the notice and had brought little Debbie in to choose her new companion and pet. Little Debbie was so excited and had decided to forgo a pink budgie, her first choice of colour, in favour of a green one. She had even chosen her new pet's name. Her Mum said that she was so excited that she was unable to sleep on the previous night.

I tried to explain to her Mum that I had been given strict instructions by my father that under no circumstances was any one to disturb his aviary and definitely never to open the bird cage door. I told Debbie and her Mum that they would have to wait a few days until the boss returned and then she and her Mum could choose a pet with my Dad, who was the keeper of the door.

On hearing this news little Debbie burst into tears sobbing inconsolably. Her Mum said that she had been so excited about the impending arrival of her first pet and she was now devastated knowing that she would have to wait another couple of days which, after all, is a long time for a little one to wait. Nobody would ever know if she took one tiny green budgie home where it would be treated with love and kindness. They said that they would even call it Harry even if it turned out to be a girl, in deference to my father.

With all this pressure I decided to take my first executive decision. After all, who would know if one tiny bird went AWOL and went to a good home? Dad would not even know. A little girl would be very happy and a relieved Mummy would tell all her friends how satisfied she was with Titanics on Waterloo Road.

Malcolm, a good friend of mine, happened to be in the shop at the time having a sandwich and overheard the anguish of this little girl. He said that he would be the knight in shining armour and would open the cage. He was over six feet tall and said that he could easily reach the door, open it, capture a budgie, a green one of course, and place it into the cage for the little girl, not forgetting to close the door afterwards. A contented tot would go home happily with her Mum. Everyone would be happy and normality would once again reign and nobody would be any the wiser.

Malcolm clambered onto a rickety chair and after a great deal of twisting and turning managed to open the door. Unfortunately being so strong he had inadvertently wrenched the little door off its hinges. I watched in horror as the birds escaped and flew in every direction all at the same time as if they had been watching an escape story from World War Two. They flew everywhere and all I could recall was Malcolm, glasses askew, shouting I've caught one clutching in his hand a little green budgie. I put Harry the bird into the cage that little Debbie had given me and ran back to the front of the shop. I gave her the new pet and I was about to explain that there had been a major mishap when fifty or so budgies flew out of the front door to freedom. The situation was becoming as ludicrous as fraught. It was like a scene from a comical *Carry On* film or a nightmare except it was real.

We tried to recapture as many birds as possible and thirty or so were recovered and placed back in the security of the cage. Where the rest went is still a mystery, but the customers complained that the chickens were very small that week! When my Dad returned home and found out, his first words were definitely not 'Who's a Cheeky Boy then'.

One of the many specials ads.

CHAPTER 7

My First Bargain

Waterloo Road in the 1960s was a fascinating mixture of chancers, entrepreneurs, hopefuls and wide boys. Everyone was trying to show the world that they were good businessmen and how successful they were. One character, who was well known in the area, would go into the local Martins bank and put £10 into his account and then add another three noughts on to his counterfoil, making it to appear as his banking that day was £10,000. He would leave the counterfoil as if by accident on the counter and would then nonchalantly leave the bank hoping that as many people as possible would see his stamped receipt and think that the boy was doing good.

Another bright spark had a very large garish red American car. He had one of his mates shoot bullet holes through the windscreen to prove to the world that he was a hard man and in league with the toughest gangsters. He was in fact a run out worker on the gaffs.

Then there was Frankie, who thought himself a Fangio who, at the time, was the world Formula One racing champion. Sadly Frankie was just the butcher driver who delivered orders for my uncle Labe in his brand new brown on brown two tone Ford Prefect van. Three forward gears and one reverse, all with synchromesh. Now Uncle Labe had purchased this van only the previous month and it was his pride and joy. He was only just learning how to drive, a new and daunting experience for anyone, let alone a middle aged man who was more *au fait* with four legged transport but, alas, never a winner.

Frankie, our racing butcher driver, had his own idea of how the Highway Code should be interpreted. This was to ignore traffic lights, halt signs and, if possible, when in traffic make his own personal lane or if that was not possible drive on the wrong side of the road. All this as fast as the poor little van would go.

In fairness to the Ford vans of that era it did pretty well, lasting a full six months before being totally clapped out. The engine, gearbox and transmission all expiring on the same day. As the van breathed its last, the unrepentant driver, so I was told, was chased up Broughton Lane by a middle aged man wearing a flat cap with a fag in his mouth waving a rather large meat cleaver at young Frankie who, fortunately for him, was not only a fast driver but also a very fast runner.

Existing in the environment of wheeler dealers and hopeful entrepreneurs encouraged me to be as sharp as the rest and have an eye for the bargain that would see me progress from a gauche youngster into a fully-fledged hard-nosed business man. I did not have to wait for long.

My father had gone to the market to buy vegetables to make up the salads for the coming week and I had been left in charge. A smartly dressed gent entered the shop and asked if Harry was around as he had a product of great interest to offer him. I told this guy that Harry was my Dad and as he was out then perhaps I could be of some assistance and help him. He told me that he had been very fortunate and had managed to acquire a quantity of olive oil and having disposed of the majority of the gallon bottles, had only twelve left. This small quantity was not enough to hawk round to the big boys and if we were interested I could buy the twelve gallons of extra virgin olive oil for £20 which, in the 1960s, was a considerable amount of money. Olive oil at that time was an expensive commodity and was fetching a premium price. The bargain seemed too good to be true so I took my first executive decision. I bought the twelve containers and paid the man twenty one pound notes. He thanked me profusely and said that in my business life I would never forget my first deal. How right he was.

When Dad returned from the market I excitedly rushed out to tell him about my first big purchase and how much profit the rare oil would bring. He opened the first container and it definitely didn't smell right. The oil in fact was rancid. Every container was the same. I had been conned. So much for Stan the lad. I felt terrible; after all, £20 was virtually a day's takings way back in the sixties. My father was not best pleased, as they say around Waterloo Road and he threatened to take the money back from my wages, which were at that time around £2/10shillings a week at five bob a time.

The oil languished for months in a dark recess of the shop as nothing was ever thrown away but it really bugged me every time I saw it. I don't know how it happened but one day near to Chanukah, the festival of lights, I had a revelation and, metaphorically speaking, I saw the light. I realised that when the religious Jews light their menorahs, the eight branched candelabras, instead of using candles they use olive oil and as previously stated, olive oil was at that time very expensive.

We bought some small plastic bottles and decanted the rancid oil into them, advertised pure olive oil fit only for the festival of lights and sold the lot, at a very healthy profit, I may add. Truly another Chanukah miracle, which I suppose I can now safely say, saved my bacon.

CHAPTER 8

To Kvetch or Not to Kvetch
That Was the Question

We had just started selling raw frozen meat and poultry in our original shop at 230 Waterloo Road but our local Jewish customers, bless them, had never lost the ability to surprise.

The vagoly had just been invented and it made the lot of the local population so much easier to do their shopping. Now a vagoly, (pronounced vague with an 'oly', tagged on the end) was a new form of transport. It was the forerunner to the Range Rovers and Audis of our now familiar Bowdon four wheel drive tractor type car (also known as Chelsea Tractors). These are seen driven at great speed and with gay abandon, seemingly by themselves, until, if you are lucky enough, you see a tiny diminutive lady attempting to peer over the steering wheel whilst on the telephone and ferrying a car full of kids to and from school or travelling to the local supermarket.

The vagoly was only two wheel drive and, in fact, was a shopping basket on wheels and was designed to stop all the schlepping involved with the every-day shopping experience. It was the bespoke Hightown form of transport and you could choose any colour as long as it was black.

This innovative invention gave the local ladies two distinct advantages: firstly the wherewithal to carry more groceries and meats than they previously had been able to do and, secondly, as going local shopping was everyone's means of communication, they could all socially congregate at the JAH Titanics on Waterloo Road for all local gossip because believe it or not, (and my grandchildren don't) the mobile phone had not been invented. Not many families had a telephone in their home, especially in local Hightown. Many of the residents did not even have mains electricity and had to rely on rechargeable accumulators from Wand and Mitchell, the electrical shop over the road. Mind you, some lucky people did have a party line. That was a shared telephone line with a neighbour, which was good for the convenience of being able to communicate with the outside world but not so good if you had nosey neighbours, as they were able to listen to your private conversations. On the positive side it was also possible for a young boy to earwig into their juicy gossip.

I digress. This new invention, the basket on wheels, arrived at the same time as our new frozen meat and poultry department. The grand sounding name of department was in fact a couple of open blue and white freezers with sliding metal lids and one was filled with chickens of various sizes. This new innovation for the kosher world filled the local girls with excitement. It was the first time that they could choose their own bird instead of the butcher bringing out from his refrigerator the chicken of his choice to sell to the customer. The only difference being that our chickens, besides being a lot cheaper to buy, were also frozen.

This posed a small problem for our dear customers, as they were always able to touch and squeeze fresh chickens, which was known colloquially as *kvetching*. I was never quite sure why they did this, but I believe that it was to see how plump that particular bird was.

Old habits and traditions die hard and can be difficult to change and the ladies and the odd gentleman who did the shopping at that time amused the staff and myself greatly as they all insisted on squeezing the frozen chickens, presumably to see if they were tender. All they got was frozen fingers. It didn't make a jot of difference as long as they all went home happy.

★

At this time I used to dread every Tuesday afternoon because it heralded the arrival of Mr. Lieberman, the well-known local shadchan, the matchmaker. Mr. Lieberman was a large figure of a man weighing in at around twenty stone. He was always dressed immaculately in a grey coat with a fur collar and a light grey suit and matching tie, a large grey Fedora hat and he wore a monocle. Not for effect, but because he could only see properly out of one eye. He always carried a large briefcase with a list of his clients.

He would search me out and beckon me over to him with an imposing large gold ring on his little finger.

'You are nineteen and it's about time we found you a nice Jewish girl to settle down with!' ….and he would then say the same thing week after week:

'Have I got a girl for you! Come and look at these beauties!'

As a 19 year old I had other thoughts on my mind regarding girls and definitely marriage was not on the agenda. Besides I told him, when the time is right I will choose my own.

He would not take a no for a satisfactory answer and insisted showing me his catalogue of beauties listed and indexed. The ugliest also being the wealthiest to the not quite as rough coming from not so rich backgrounds. When I remonstrated with him about their lack of aesthetic beauty, he would say beauty is always in the eye of the beholder and beside it was the inner beauty that mattered most. He would tell me that I did not have to look at them very often, just do the odd *mitzvah* by them and I would have a very pleasant and easy life style.

I was not at all convinced and week after week would beg him not to show me anymore. Thankfully he eventually gave me up as a no hoper. He would say that I had no soul and could suffer dire consequences later when I had made my own choice and not relied on his expertise. Eventually I took my chance and am still awaiting the dire consequences, or am I still suffering them?

WE ARE PLEASED TO ANNOUNCE
THAT OUR NEW
CHICKEN 'KVETCHERY'
IS NOW FULLY OPERATIONAL

Empire a la carte whole chickens .... 75p lb.
Empire a la carte cut up chicken   £1.49 per 2lb box
Empire Pastrami (Turkey) .... 49p pkt.
Aviv egg matzos .... 49p pkt.
Rakusen matzos .... 55p pkt.
Yehuda matzos .... 89p pkt.
Rakusen tub margarine (sunflower) 22p or 5 for £1
Telma tub margarine 29p
Tomor .... 75p lb.
Gouda cheese .... £1.59 lb.
Cottage cheese plain/flavoured 39p/42p
Family size crisps .... 35p or 3 for £1.00
Bennetts Mayonnaise 59p
Tomato purée cartons 18p
Mini/maxi Mandles snaxstix 45p
Planters sleeves nuts (4 assorted pkts.) 49p
Osem Assorted puddings etc. 25p
Bennetts salad dressings 49p
Rakusen biscuits (creams) 25p
Rakusen biscuits (shortcake) 25p
Rakusen biscuits (digestive) 35p
Rakusen biscuits (nice) 33p
Broken kosher biscuits .... 19p ½lb.
Matzo meal medium/fine .... 39p lb.
Vermicelli broad/fine .... 35p ½lb.
Californian prunes .... 39p per ½lb. pkt.
Osem assorted soups 52p
Krakus cucumbers 60p
Large jars sour cucumbers 49p
Mazchix 75p
1 litre vegetable oil 89p
4 litre vegetable oil £3.59
1 litre orange juice 29p
Skrek soups .... 3 for £1.00
Sides smoked salmon (approx. 1¼lb) ..... £2.89 lb
Cocktail pieces, smoked salmon .... £1.19 ½lb.
Frozen buttered kipper fillets/mackerel 35p
4 cod in butter £1.36
Jars Dutch herring 59p
Danish herrings 79p/89p
Tins Israeli apple juice 35p
2 litre lemonade 49p
Diet coke/orange .... 3 for 49p
Plaice/haddock/cod fillets .... 79p lb
Hake fillets .... 89p lb.
2lb Birds Eye peas 85p
Tin mackerel 19p
Elswood herrings 99p
Chrain 42p
Israeli Turkey schnitzels .... 4 for £1.89
Jus Rol puff pastry 49p
Israeli tin corn 39p
Israeli grapefruit juice natural 13p
No. 1 size, white eggs .... £1.99 tray 30
Candles 12/20 .... 69p

Our price list ad.

44

CHAPTER 9

Car and Consequences

My very first car was a bright red mini registration number 6079 NC, which was bought for me, not out of love but necessity as that ensured that I would be able to arrive at work at a respectable time and not rely on the 26 bus that stopped outside number 230 Waterloo Road. This served me well but after two years of being abused by a young aggressive driver it was time to change. Besides it was not a good pulling car and as history proved the next was not only a great pulling car but was also my metaphoric gelding. I digress.

The new Triumph Spitfire had just been launched and I fell in love and was allowed to enter into negotiations for one. Now in the 1960s, although car salesmen are the descendants of horse thieves, in those days they posed as gentlemen and instead of going to the garage they would come to you and test your car, give you a price and shake hands on the deal. You would then count your fingers and if all was OK proceed.

One bright Monday morning Mr Freeman of Hollingdrake's of Stockport came to inspect my Mini with a view to swapping it for a Spitfire. He duly jumped into the mini to take it on a test drive to determine the part-ex value for a deal, taking into account that a Triumph spitfire was £702. This included a heater as an extra. He returned from his test drive, me waiting anxiously on the pavement outside the shop. He opened the door without looking in the mirror, and a bus knocked the door off, smashing the front wing and writing off the car. Thankfully Mr Freeman was unhurt. I was then the proud owner of the very first Spitfire in Manchester, at a very special price!

This car served me well in my pulling days but became my subsequent downfall because one of these young beauties was lured, not by me but my car and having deliberated with friends into buying flat shoes, she hooked me and we are still together some fifty years later.

CHAPTER 10

Manchester Jewish Butchers

The Manchester Jewish Butchers was an organisation which embraced the whole of the trade, including butchers & meat manufacturers. The idea was that everyone had equal rights and that as a group they were able to buy meat competitively, be treated fairly and the larger shops looked after the smaller. This was great in theory but in practice it was war; you had to be alert at all times. I remember my Dad saying that dealing with them was like working with a barrel of monkeys.

When I first started work there were thirty eight shops spread across Manchester. The figurehead, who was secretary of this august body, was Lazzie Snowise. Now Lazzie ruled the butchers with an iron fist. He would not stand for any nonsense from any one. He would buy the meat from the abattoirs and not only distribute it but also deal with the Manchester Beth Din, who were in charge of all beef, lamb, chickens and so on, being kosher and acceptable to the community. That's where the fun began.

Every butcher placed his order on a Sunday. The beef and lamb would be loaded onto a truck, usually on a Tuesday and Wednesday. It was at this point that labels on the beef were sometimes changed so this could mean that someone who was bunging the driver would get either better weight or better quality beef than their rivals. The livers were also swapped and so on and so on. It was, metaphorically speaking, a kosher rat race and also in this mix was the odd treife liver scandal…. treife being not Kosher and definitely not allowed.

The butcher's week started on Tuesday when the meat was delivered and had to be worked on. Wednesday and Thursday were the two busiest days for selling in the shop or for deliveries. Friday was always a short day because it was the start of the Sabbath and the women would all be cooking for their families. Sunday was a day for collecting the debts from the previous week and sometimes some more, especially if there had been extra liver in the order and the husband was out.

Monday was paying bills day. Remember, no pay no meat. After payments there was either a card school at the butchers' office or off to the bookies to have a bet and the whole cycle would be repeated.

Writing about the Manchester Butchers reminds me of the birth of Tovah Meats, the legitimate child of the Manchester Butchers Trading Society. This was to be the most exciting, forward thinking project for the Manchester butchers and it could and should have been. It was the brainchild of Lazzie and his idea was to build a central factory where all the meat would be processed, the raw meat distributed to the butchers according to their requirements and the off cuts and all unwanted meats made up into salamis, sausages, blocks of pressed beef, pickled tongues, and so on, to be sold in all the shops. Any surplus was to be sold on to the caterers, schools and any shops or stores which wanted to buy these products.

To make it work was theoretically simple and essentially brilliant: there was no need for thirty eight shops. Ten or twelve supermarket type shops would be opened, on either existing sites or new custom built ones across Manchester stretching from Whitefield in the north to Cheadle in the south. At that time Cheadle was considered as the Golden Medina, a new and exciting territory south of the Irwell where North Manchester religious Jews had not and still don't venture. Not everyone was scared of the North/South divide and the South side began to flourish.

The simple solution was that the guys whose shops were to be closed would work in the factory, not altogether menial but administration, production, management and general supervision. The stores that were left would be run by the shop owners but as a partnership with all thirty eight butchers. The savings would be enormous, saving on some twenty properties, vans, staff, and so on, but still retaining their entire customer base.

The distribution of profits was easily worked out as it was to be based on everyone's average weekly meat and poultry sales over the previous two years and divided up percentage wise so no one would be worse off but everyone would benefit. Every butcher was asked to contribute to this new and exciting venture, the more you contributed the bigger the share and dividend you would receive. The average was £1000 per butcher.

A brand new factory was designed and approved by all and was built in Collingham Street, next door to the chicken factory, so named Collingham Quality Foods, but that's another epic story. While the factory was being built life continued as normal. Meat would be sent processed and sold week in and week out. To ensure loyalty several things were used. One of them was a dividend based on your meat turnover over the previous year's trading. This was distributed at the event of the year, The Manchester Jewish Butchers Dinner and Dance.

This was always at The Holmes in Sedgley Park Road and catered by Mrs Fruhman. This was a truly *grob* (translation on request) dinner, the women in all their finery, every one of them trying to outdo the other, flaunting the biggest diamond rings, jewellery and furs that readies could buy. Beryl Cook could have had inspiration from this assembly. The dinners were magnificent. Chefs carving huge ribs of beef, tongues and every cut of meat and lamb imaginable. The wine and whisky flowed all night and envelopes were distributed. The dividend! These were put in handbags, secreted down ample cleavages, some for spending on family holidays, on house maintenance and some, alas, for paying off the bookies. It was always an interesting and eventful night, a night to remember.

The magnificent factory, duly completed, started producing cooked meats and distributing them. A meeting was called to finalise the purchasing of new shops and the closing down of some of the existing ones as approved in the previous year.

Then a funny incident happened. I am not sure whose wife asked the question but it had a profound effect and was the eventual ruination of the Manchester butchers dream that would have made every one of the Manchester butchers very wealthy.

The question was: If you work in the factory how can I acquire cash to buy my shoes and clothes as I will not be able to put my hand in the till?? And that was that!!

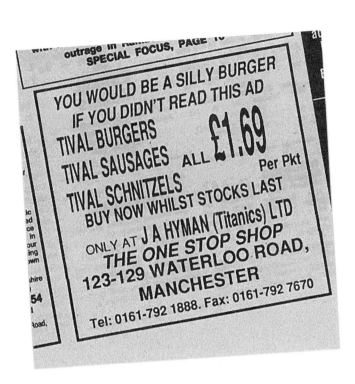

Silly Burgers ad.
The Jewish Telegraph.

CHAPTER 11

The Bone Man

One weekly event was the arrival of the bone man. You knew when he was nearby especially in the summer as his truck would trundle up with the most delicious of aromas, especially for the flies. He would then empty our bone bins, weigh the bones, pay us £2 /10s for them and then take them to the glue factory where they would be melted down and used for the glue in making envelopes. I often wondered how many vegetarians or the more religious members of the community knew this when they had a good lick to fasten their envelopes. The monies collected would be put away and would go towards our annual holiday.

My, have times changed. Nowadays we pay them to take the bones. This was the result of mad cow disease. Millions of cattle were slaughtered just in case. In case of what? No one quite knew and still are not quite sure. So all these cows died along with tens of thousands of starving people in Africa, who I am sure, if they would have been consulted, would have taken their chances of contracting mad cow disease but they were not and thousands died of starvation.

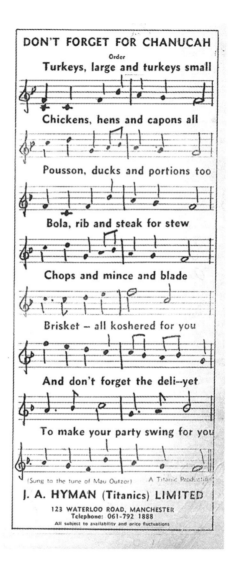

This is a Chanucah ad sung to the tune of Maoz Tzur – A traditional Chanucah song.

54

CHAPTER 12

Pesach (Passover)

The climax of the year and the most scary of all, was Pesach. I still mention the P word with fear and trepidation. To put a myth to rest, we did not make shed loads of money. It was OK but the amount of effort and hard graft that went into this mammoth project was more of a tribute to our ancestors leaving Egypt for the Promised Land, which at some point seemed like Waterloo Road.

Pesach used to be a sensible festival, food wise. The list in 1975 had 50 items on it. The basics: cheese, unsalted butter and chocolate liqueurs from Ringers of Holland, chocolates and sweets from Israel, matzos from Bonns of Carlisle and sometimes, when shalom was made with the Beth Din, Rakusens matzos and crackers. Oil was from a new can and was decanted into new bottles. New packs of sugar, salt and certain spices were allowed. Dried fruits, jams and honey and that, basically, was your lot. Life was a lot less complicated. Now commercialism has overtaken the real meaning of the spirit of this festival and we have hundreds of items, most so obscure you wouldn't eat them during the year so why at Pesach?

The logistics of organising for Pesach were enormous. Let me try to explain, so the next time some wise guy tells me that you just stand there and take the money he may understand a little more. Three months before P one had to place the order making sure there was enough of each product, too much and you would be stuck with the goods afterwards and who wants a packet of almond macaroons after Pesach? (Come to think of it, who really wants one during Pesach?)

When the goods were delivered they had to be priced. Too expensive and the customer would shop elsewhere, too cheap and you would be working for nothing. The clever thing was to be cheaper than the competition and still make a profit. Secrecy, surprise, zany advertising and most of all, very hard work. A huge problem was deliveries. It was easy to order the goods but our Jewish wholesalers seemed to have a *ma□ana* philosophy and having to clear, clean the shop and factory and wait for deliveries was a bit fraught, to say the least. This was not withstanding the sometimes obscure rulings of our Beth Din, which seemed to become more paranoid every year.

We had to fit six weeks takings in two weeks. This sounds great but for four weeks afterwards nothing much happened as we were closed a lot of the time due to the holidays and also people were sick of eating so much. So all in all, Pesach was a very stressful time. As someone told me, (and who am I to disagree?) it was like having PMT for three months at a time.

There were some lighter moments, which made Pesach bearable. There was the time when this young, innocent, pretty little girl, resplendent in school uniform was introduced to the mad house, doing Pesach shopping with Mummy Sonya, for the very first time. Little Beverley heard the dreaded F word, not I may add, directed at her or her lovely Mum, but at some lady who kept poking her finger into my arm and asking the age old question: was the matzos fresh, was the steaming hot chopped fish fresh? This F incident cost me a box of chocolates for the poor lady and a bag of sweets for little Bev, who never forgot where she learnt her very first swear word. Every time I see her now we still giggle over that time, many years ago.

There was the time when a zany, bubbly lady from Southport brought her two daughters to their Passover initiation ceremony at 123 Waterloo Road, resplendent in mink coat, armed with 3 lists, one for her Mum, one for her sister and one for her. She sent the girls off in different directions for the separate orders. Alas, the best laid plans in the middle of a balagan went somewhat awry. A dead certainty, as it was hard enough making up one order at a time and this hard headed business lady was reduced to tears. Sitting in the middle of the floor, mink dishevelled, with tins and packages all around her and her two daughters looking at her in astonishment at the prospect that this is what they had to do in years to come. It couldn't have been so bad, as one of the girls, young Ginger, subsequently became my daughter-in-law, but later tragically was taken away from us, without me really getting to know her.

CHAPTER 13

J.A. Hyman – The Centre of the World

Serving the Community

In the 70's, Manchester became the swag centre of the world or so it seemed. All of a sudden, like an explosion, like a mushroom growth, Bury New Road was reborn. The old run down Jewish shops selling bespoke suits and suit lengths, as well as the two kosher wholesalers Goldsteins and Habers, all cashed in on this regeneration, one moving to Great Cheetham Street East and the other to Swinton.

The area was the first conglomeration of different cultures and religions, all opening warehouses to stake their claims as fast as possible to cash in on this new metaphorical gold rush. The old Yiddisher shopkeepers and owners of dilapidated buildings in Bury New Road must have thought that their birthday had arrived early.

Properties in the area were selling for up to five or six times their real worth. As the old Jews moved out the Indians and young Jewish entrepreneurs moved in, making up Manchester's first area of multicultural society. There was a market on every Sunday morning in Bury New Road and one had to be up very early in order to have a good pitch.

Some wanted Bury New Road to be renamed as The Delhi New Road, as this new industry was run mainly by Asians. It put Manchester on the map as far as market traders and shopkeepers were concerned. The whole area was revitalised and the 'Boys' opened wholesale warehouses in the surrounding areas, Derby Street, Broughton Street, Waterloo Road and all the roads near our best known local landmark, namely Strangeways prison.

Where did we fit into this equation? Well, quite simply, location. The traders came from all over the UK to buy their wares from bedding to hardware and that's where we became involved. Let me explain: Melvyn from Sheffield, for example, would come to Manchester every Tuesday to buy goods for his shop or market stall. After completing his buying, he would come in to our store where he could use the loos and believe me, as one gets older one appreciates a facility like this, wash off the grime of Manchester 8, have a sandwich and buy his meat and delicatessen to take back home.

This, however, was a world before instant communication. Mobile phones had not been invented, so quite simply JAH became, yet again, the centre of the universe. The only way Melvyn could be contacted was a telephone call to us and the message would be put on a notice board. For example, a special order or a line had run out and had to be replaced. This must have saved hundreds if not thousands of pounds in missed sales as there was no other way of being contacted. Thus we became the halfway house and became the focal point for all the buyers who, besides being customers, became friends.

This resurgence of the area was great for business and we therefore decided to open a snack bar to adequately feed all our hungry customers and to send them on their way with a full tummy so they were ready and able to wheel and deal and trade in the afternoon. Always remember: never do business on an empty stomach.

They, whoever they are, say that you never forget your first time. Our first day was amazing. Great approval from sated and satisfied customers. We had employed a Polish lady by the name of Helen, who was a big girl with an even bigger smile. The shop at 230 Waterloo Road had a large area and one third had been requisitioned for the snack bar cum café cum restaurant. We were able to sit around twenty-five very hungry people and boy, did they all have hearty appetites. It must be a universally accepted fact that all wives keep their menfolk on special diets and healthy foods. This was great as they could break out from their metaphorical shackles and eat real man food, proper haimishe food; food full of taste and smaltz. In fact, the café should have been called 'Calories and Cholesterol at Titanics on Waterloo Road'.

Helen made the best holoshkies - that is boiled cabbage leaves stuffed with mincemeat and rice. Her potato latkes were the talk of the town, but always the traditional favourite was hot salt beef, plenty of fat round the edges of course and chips with plenty of salt and vinegar and a pickled sweet and sour cucumber served with lashings of mustard.

Her crowning glory, however, was the apple strudel. It was so good that people would telephone to reserve a piece. Some fifty years on and I can still savour and salivate over that amazing taste. Looking back I suppose that this food was a heart attack served on a plate.

All of this was served by a very pretty and extremely sexy girl named Maria, who was definitely as much of an attraction as the latkes and was the focus of many of the men's attention. Our Maria was not with us for very long, as many wives had objected to this singularly attractive lady being paid way too many lecherous glances from their various husbands.

As the café became busier, my Aunt Edna was asked to help and to steady the Titanics boat and to make it more wife acceptable. Aunty Edna was my mum's younger sister and she helped with running the café for years, including moving from the spiritual home at number 230 to the new shop further down the road, where the café moved up the stairs where one could savour the stunning views of Strangeways prison and north Manchester.

When Helen our lovely cook decided to hang up her pinny and retire, we were then very fortunate in finding a wonderful and colourful replacement cook by the name of Olwyn.

Now Olwyn had hailed originally from Jamaica and was a wonderful exponent of West Indian food. She had the canny knack of converting recipes from her home country into the kosher equivalent. Her cooking was hot and spicy, just like her temperament, and woe betide any customer who had the temerity to complain about any of her dishes. She would tower above them and demand to know what the problem was? The customer would always back down and apologise, as she constantly carried a rolling pin with her at all times.

'Tools of the trade' she would say.

These performances attracted a lot of attention and I am sure that customers would come in just to see our Olwyn in full flow. She cooked for us until we moved down the road some two years later, when she decided that it was time to hang up her apron and stow away her rolling pin. That lady was certainly great at her cooking and had performed and entertained our clientele to such an extent that on her final day all the customers applauded her and bought her a huge bouquet of flowers.

Olwyn's successor was a fiery Italian lady named Carmella. Her forte was, of course, pasta dishes. Carmella made fresh pasta every day and her spaghetti and meatballs were soon the talk of the town. She taught everyone, that is customers and staff, how to swear in Italian and with meat balls and pasta sauce flying around it made for interesting dining.

When the café cum snack bar duly had run its natural course, the reasons for its final demise were twofold: the first being that life was changing and people were always in too much of a hurry to enjoy leisurely lunches. The age of technology had started the modern era: everyone rushing, things becoming instant, no time to eat and think, everything was different. For the better or worse? Make up your own minds. I often wonder: are computers a blessing or a modern day curse?

Secondly our staff were helping themselves to their lunch and what had started out as a perk to make sure that all the cooked food that was surplus at the end of each day was used up had now become a right. The girls were now cooking for the staff. We were running out of food before paying customers could get their lunches. Enough was enough, or basta e basta, as Carmella would have said. But it was all great fun while it lasted. We had been serving lunches for nearly twenty years and people have fond memories and still reminisce of all the calories and cholesterol consumed at Waterloo Road.

The Titanics price list ad.

CHAPTER 14

Hy-Fry – The Laughing Fish

In 1975 or thereabouts we started making chopped fish mix; which was a mixture of all of the raw ingredients needed to make chopped and fried or boiled fishcakes. Until then, housewives had always made their own. With less time on their hands, now becoming equal with their menfolk, going out to work and, figuratively speaking, burning their bras there was less time to go to the fishmonger, take the fish home, skin and mince it, and then add ingredients. The fish mix saved them all this and they could just add whatever they wanted to make their own taste and no one would be any the wiser.

This product started in a small way and suddenly, overnight, took off, catching us completely by surprise. Amazed, we had to think of a name for this wonder product. My Dad and I came up with the marvellous name of Hy-Fry, simple but perfect and the logo incorporated this in the shape of a fish which is still used today. The problem with this product was acquiring enough raw product at the correct price.

One day, and I am still not sure how we were found, we received a phone call from some guy called Reg who said he could and would be able to supply us with the very best quality fish at ridiculously cheap prices. Were we interested? You bet we were!

The Hy-Fry logo

Reg was based near Grimsby and was the owner of a mink farm. Now as it happened Reg was buying all the best grade off cuts from the major fish processors in the area. Their problem evidently was when the fish was cut by bandsaw for the fish finger trade there were always offcuts. These offcuts were considered to be unusable as they were the wrong shape, although exactly the same quality as their more illustrious cod fish fingers. In fact, it was the same product without their coating on. These were taken off the assembly line and virtually given to Reg at a daft price. He realised that this product was far too good to serve to his mink, besides there was virtually an endless supply, and that's where we came in to the equation. Over a period of eight years we sent a van to Grimsby every week to buy this fish. We didn't care if it was all odd pieces as we were going to mince it anyway. Every week my darling wife abandoned her children and drove to London in a Cortina Estate laden with Hy-Fry fish mix, in insulated boxes, to a lovely gentleman in Golders Green called Mr Bell, who sold them on to all the local London stores. Jennifer would then go to the newly opened Brent Cross shopping centre and recharge her batteries with a little retail therapy and drive back home to Manchester. All in a day.

Reg and family became very good friends of ours. In fact, forty of his finest mink sacrificed themselves for Jennifer's fortieth birthday present, one for every year. Thankfully it was not for her sixty-fifth. I would be still paying.

Everything was going great. Then one day I received a desperate phone call from Reg. It was all over. The fish factories had realised that they could use this waste product themselves to make mince fish fingers and that was the end. Thankfully it had taken them eight years to make this startling discovery so our gravy train came to a fishy end, but Hy-Fry lives on.

CHAPTER 15

In Search of a Battered Sole

Now Reg was always thinking of new angles on how to make money and I had mentioned on several occasions that we should try and explore the magical world of kosher fish fingers, which would tie in nicely with our Hy-Fry fish mix.

What made a fish finger kosher as opposed to not kosher was that the fish had to have the usual fins and scales. To prove this to our religious authorities Reg told me that he had discovered a factory that would conform to all the regulations that would be required. The problem was that the factory was in the town of Aarus in Denmark. He would be able to arrange transport to the factory and all we needed was a Rabbi. I had the very guy and he was small as well, which was good just in case the means of transport wasn't very big, because as well as the Rabbi we had to fit in his large hat.

The day duly arrived and at five o'clock in the morning I called at the door of our supervising Rabbi who duly answered the door and as he was leaving the house I saw a figure at the window, his missus, who shouted,

'Take care tataler and do not go on any dangerous small aeroplanes'.

I said nothing but sped off in the direction of Grimsby airport. Or should I say, airstrip.

At about six thirty, on reaching the services somewhere near Hull, I was informed by my passenger that he had discovered that very morning, in my car, the answer to something that he had been studying for years. When I asked him what it was he told me that after years of research, (and I had no reason to doubt him), that it was possible to kosher enamel surfaces and thus enable them to be used for Passover. I feel proud to think that this revelation came to this momentous result, in my car on this of all mornings. He also wanted to daven; that is, say his morning prayers before we reached our rendezvous.

When our Rabbi started praying he created quite a stir in the Hull /Grimsby fish trucking circles as I had parked in the commercial vehicle park and these gentlemen were not used to seeing a Rabbi in full flow, so to speak. They soon had the gist of the morning prayers and even joined in to say amen at the appropriate times!

Our Rabbi, having done his devotions for the morning now needed to eat, his good lady wife having provided more than adequate fare for him. He needed to wash his hands, this being for two reasons, firstly hygiene and secondly religious. The nearest source of water was the river Calder and I held on to his coat-tail as he clambered down the bank. I often wondered what would have happened if I had let go, but I digress.

After breakfast, that was his, not mine, we proceeded to the Humberside airfield where we were met by our host, Reg. Our Rabbi, on seeing only a tiger moth type airplane with four seats, including the pilot, tried to run for home and flee but he was trapped. I have often thought over the years that a distinguished Rabbi, who could even determine the qualities of enamel, would not have his faith in the Lord to protect him. He said that I had reassured his wife and, of course, himself that it was a large plane with lots of engines, not one. Eventually the pilot reassured him that it was quite safe and that he was sober so we took off.

The flight to Denmark took about two hours, our rabbi studying and Reg eating his very appetising sandwiches. His wife had made extra for me but although they had nothing offensive like ham or any sort of meat and were only mouth-watering cheese and pickle, I had to decline, as they were not strictly kosher, though I was starving. I was going to ask Reg to save me some but, unable to communicate he ate them all, much to my consternation.

We duly arrived at the factory, which turned out to be modern and state of the art. They had said that they would go along with any recommendations from the rabbinate to make a kosher production for our Hy-Fry fish fingers. All we had to do was to give them a time and date. We were then offered refreshments that looked wonderful but I politely declined, although by this time I felt on the verge of starvation. Everyone tucked in, including the rabbi with his own packed lunch prepared for him, presumably by his devoted wife. I was becoming desperate for food.

My lucky break came finally as we went back to the airstrip. Our rabbi went to use the facilities and I noticed in the little café in the airport the last Danish pastry on a tray. Now saint I may not be, but starving I was and before you could say Rabbi W the pastry was bought and eaten and as our distinguished clergyman reappeared I was already removing the crumbs from my person.

Going home in our little craft our driver the pilot offered round a bottle of whisky for everyone to toast a seemingly successful day. When it came to my turn I was just about to place the bottle to my lips when our rear passenger, the Rabbi told me that I had to say aloud the prayer for whisky (we have a prayer for everything in our religion). Luckily I knew it and after the appropriate amen thankfully had a swig.

We arrived safe and sound in Grimsby and took our visitor back home to his wife and children. She seemed so relieved to see him that one could have thought that he had been kidnapped.

We never were given permission to use that factory to make us our fish fingers, although they would have accommodated all the demands, criteria and idiosyncrasies of our religious leaders. Maybe it was because we did not pay the necessary ransom.

BATTERED COD TURNS UP FROZEN IN HIGHTOWN

BY OUR SPECIAL REPORTER

Who also found:

Sides Smoked Salmon ... £2.29 lb.	
(approx. 1½ lb.)	
Battered Cod	59p lb.
Breaded Cod	59p lb.
Fillets Cod	59p lb.
Fillets Haddock	59p lb.
Jumbo Fish Fingers	59p lb.
Salmon, Trout	59p lb.
Breaded Sole	59p lb.
Broken Fish Fingers	24½p lb.
(per 2 lb.)	
Salmon 3/5 lb., gutted	£1.49 lb.
Cod in Sauce . 29p or 10 for £2.75	
Pkts. Smoked Salmon ... 69p ¼ lb.	
Krakus Cucumber	53p
Israeli Turkey Schnitzell	
£1.69 per four	
Trays of Eggs (30)	99p

AND NOW SOMETHING NEW

Frozen Cauliflower	34½p lb.
Frozen Sprouts	28p lb.
Frozen Beans	29½p lb.
Frozen Peas	22½p lb.
Frozen Carrots	22½p lb.
(All per 2 lb. pack)	
Empire Turkey Dinners	75p
Empire Potato Knishes	49p
Aviv Matzo	55p
Israeli Candles (20)	69p
Refills, three for	50p
4 litre Vegetable Oil	£2.19
4 litre Corn Oil	£3.29
1 litre Vegetable Oil	59p
Israeli Orange Juice, litre jar	50p

THE 'CHEEPEST' KOSHERED ROASTER & BOILER PORTIONS IN TOWN
AND THE KINDEST CUT OF ALL . . . READY KOSHERED MEAT

All available at

J. A. Hyman Ltd. (Titanics)

Who else!

123 WATERLOO ROAD   **Tel.: 061-792 1888**

(All offers subject to availability)

CHAPTER 16

The Complete Whine Shop

The complete kosher store was the one that provided a complete range of foods for the Jewish household. We were not quite all there, or should I phrase it differently, we were not yet selling the complete package for our clientele.

What we needed to sell to complement our comprehensive range of both raw and cooked meats, fish products, breads and, of course, delicatessen was logically wines and the odd spirit. Up until this time Jews and wine did not seem to be compatible.

The only wines that were sold to the Jewish community were the Palwin Nos. 10, 11, 4 and 4a. Now the name Palwin was in itself interesting as the name and trade mark Palwin originated from The Palestine Wine Company, being the first three letters of each name. The Kiddush wines numbers 10, 11, 4 and 4A were the numbers of the buses that passed the factory at that time, so I have been told. Not really very romantic but very practical.

At Passover and on special occasions Advocaat and, of course, cherry brandy were also drank. In fact, Auntie Lilly, when really fancying a tipple at a wedding or any family celebration, used to pour a drop of cherry brandy into an eye bath size glass of Advocaat and this was called a bleeding heart. The cherry brandy seemed to sit on top of the Advocaat, seemingly to become heart shaped. Thus the name… but I digress.

At that time Jews with wine was something of a joke. When someone was asked what Jewish wine was, he answered without hesitation: 'My wife veining (moaning) that you don't take me to Marbella? Why can't I have diamonds like my next door neighbour? Why can't I have a Volvo?' and so on.

It was time to change all this and educate the local community to the benefits of wine drinking and that there was life after Palwin.

People were now travelling to foreign parts and were beginning to appreciate good wines and to realise that it did not need to be sweet to be good. Wines were being developed in Israel and they were being improved all the time. I thought it a good idea, to support Israeli Kosher wines because at this time they were virtually the only grape related alcohol we were allowed to buy, as they had to be deemed as kosher for us to be able to sell them.

An executive decision having been made, it was decided that we apply for a wine and spirit licence, which should be a formality as we were a family store knowing all our clientele and not being open in the evenings.

How wrong I was. Having applied to the council, they were less than happy to be cooperative. I began to wonder what their problem was, as all the other ethnic stores opening up in the Cheetham area of Manchester seemed to have been given licences pretty easily. With us they eventually decided to send in the full monty of the Manchester licensing committee, presumably to see if we were fit to sell ethnic wines and the odd bottle of spirit.

Imagine my surprise when one Tuesday morning a forty-seater coach rolled onto our forecourt and the entire committee flooded in. The questions that were asked regarding the strategic placing of the alcohol in the shop seemed to figure predominately in their minds as they did not want the booze to be accessible to minors. I tried to explain that we did not have young customers, as this was a family store and children never visited the shop alone, only with their mums and or dads and the odd time with a doting grandparent. We were definitely not a convenience store. Also the locals were not interested in Kiddush wines or anything that was Jewish and we were never used by the locals except for the odd bread and occasional candles. The candles being used presumably for séances, or some other weird or strange doings.

This inspection went on for at least an hour and as they finally started to leave one of the committee, a lady of the blue rinse brigade, asked one of the girls for a quarter of pickled meat for her tea. She said that she might as well do a bit of shopping as she put it, whilst in the field. When she went to the till to pay I said that we would treat her to her tea and, as a bit of fun, because of the enormity of the committees operation in trying to crack the proverbial nut with a sledgehammer, I told her that we would not charge for the four ounces of pressed beef so that she should view us favourably when the license would be debated. I thought that this was funny but somehow the humour of the situation seemed to be missing with this lady. She was not amused.

We eventually were given the wine and spirit licence with the proviso that the bottles were on shelves at least thirty six inches from the floor. One can form one's own judgement as to why the height from the floor was so important because I had no idea and when I later asked that specific question neither had anybody else.

CHAPTER 17

Fish Fressing Competition

Isn't it funny how seemingly great ideas sometimes go awry and the end results seem to bounce back and bite you on the bum?

Always searching for new angles and constantly racking my brain on how to come up with zany and funny ideas, I suddenly had an inspiration: 'Let's have a chopped and fried fish fressing (eating) competition!' This appeared to be inspirational. Who else could or would have thought of a fish fressing comp? The *Guinness Book of Records* was consulted and were not particularly interested. The Beth Din weren't too keen to send adjudicators either so it was decided to do the judging in-house so to speak.

First prize was to be the Titanics trophy. This was to be an annual event and the winner's name would be engraved on the cup and he or she would be the fish fresser of the year and be entitled to hold the trophy for twelve months.

An entry form was placed in that famous and now defunct journal, namely The Jewish Gazette, as well as forms in the shop. The comp was to be on a Wednesday evening and hopefully there would be a great deal of interest from the local Jewish public as eating was always very close to their hearts, especially chopped and fried fish.

There was an underwhelming number of contestants who had entered if I recall, some ten in all. There were a few pros, who had clearly been practising for years. The bookies' choice and firm favourite was a certain zip seller and chazzan, MF, with one of the best voices ever to have graced a Manchester Synagogue. However, most contestants were the local dossers, who were up for a free meal and had seen the ad in the Gazette, presumably whilst eating their fish and chips, the Jewish Gazette being the perfect size for wrapping up chips as well as other things.

The rules were very simple: the winner being the person who ate the most fish balls in five minutes and the judge's decision, being me, was final. The great day arrived and my wonderful Salford fish fryers, whose colourful story will be told at some later stage, stayed late and fried a mountain of delicious, dark brown, crispy, heavenly smelling chopped-fried fish.

The contestants lined up around the mound of fish balls. After they had washed and said the correct prayers the whistle sounded and off they went. They never had a chance. MF the singing zip seller, won by at least ten fish balls from the second contestant. The bookies are always right. The favourite had won. His prize: the cup and a packet of Rennies. Well done MF!

Now, what began as a bit of a joke ended in that other Jewish journal, The Jewish Telegraph. If I recall, the letter columns were full of complaints of greed and gluttony and condemnation for the competition but it was still good fun to put on. It's these little bits of nonsense that make everyday life more exciting.

Another occasion that backfired was when we were asked to sponsor a Junior Stage 80 production, which was and still is a local and highly successful Jewish Theatre Group. The show being an adaptation of Sweeny Todd, the scheming murdering barber. I had to try and think of something in keeping with the production, which would advertise our name and products and was in the spirit and the ethos of the show. There was also one of my children involved and that added to the pressure.

It was a logical conclusion that in the spirit of the show we would make one of our specialities of the day, meat pies otherwise known as growlers. Growlers were so called because it was said that after gobbling them down some thirty minutes or so later they would make a rumbling sound in one's tummy. This was pure fantasy and was so named by one of my uncles, after he had eaten a pie one day much too quickly but the name growler stuck and the meat pies are still described as such by some of us older ones even today.

After Mr. S Todd had started with his dark and dastardly deeds, making his little victims into pies, there was to be an interval. The cast would then throw to the audience beautifully wrapped J.A. Hyman meat pies, advertising the name and this delicious product. Now as it was Junior Stage 80, the young version of the Jewish Theatre Group, the advertising seemed relevant to the play and appealed to my oddball sense of humour. It read: 'Kosher meat pies made from Jewish children'. Everything, as far as I was concerned went down well. The audience was greatly appreciative having a freebie and everyone went home fully satisfied culturally after a super show and a tummy full of growler.

The crits in the JT were full of praise for the show but the letters from a few people, some being survivors of the holocaust, thought that the description and implication of the meat pies was in poor taste. I suppose that they had a point but it was all done in the spirit of fun.

CHAPTER 18

A Prickly Situation

Way back in the seventies, that's the 1970s, new goods were arriving daily. The general public having been educated in the new foods after holidays, as travel had become easier and people had become far more adventurous in their culinary tastes. Items like hoummous, tahini and falafel appeared on the shelves of the local shops and were becoming more and more popular with the customers as were poultry and turkey products from Israel.

It had not always been like that. We Ashkenazi are a traditional lot and were very conservative in our foods. The preparation, the mode of cooking had all been passed down by our great grandparents and grandparents from the villages and towns of whichever empire they lived in at that time. One year they would be Russians, the next Poles or Austrians: no stability, no rights, they were the serfs of every ruling body; the downtrodden flotsam of central Europe and they were poor. Persecuted by the tyrants and Cossacks of central Europe, not being allowed to own land and barely being able to survive on a day to day basis had taught them to be not only frugal but to be magicians with the meagre food that they had at their disposal.

My grandma could conjure up a banquet from virtually nothing. Give her a chicken, an onion and couple of carrots and two hours later this was turned into Jewish penicillin. Grandma's chicken soup, the veritable elixir of life. The fat would be carefully decanted and mixed with flour and spices, stuffed into the skin at the neck end, sown up lovingly with cotton. This amazingly tasty killer was aptly named helzel and the whole boiled, cooked chicken rescued from the soup was ritually roasted with potatoes in chicken fat and served up.

These dinners tasted delightful, and were definitely not bad for you, as calories had not yet been invented. Potatoes were shredded with a ribheizer, a grater for the uninformed. An egg, grated onion and a large dollop of chicken smaltz were all placed in a kugel teppel, a large enamel bowl and baked in the oven until golden brown on top. The test of a good potato kugel was the amount of chicken fat that would ooze out when a spoon was pressed down onto it. This was definitely a heart attack waiting to happen disguised, alas, as delicious tasting food.

Beetroots were shredded, boiled and made into soup called borscht. At Passover for a special treat, these very same beetroots were shredded along with lemons and sugar, boiled up in a large pot and were made into a conserve known as eingemacht, or beet and lemon jam. Candy was made from grating carrots, adding sugar, lemon juice and ground ginger, boiled up in a large metal pot, preferably copper, rolled out into trays and when cooled down, cut into squares. This candy was called ingber. Herrings were minced along with apple, breadcrumbs and sugar. This was called chopped herring.

There are many more examples of the inventiveness of our grandmas. Making many meatballs out of a tiny piece of meat and more. The traditional foods that were handed down were a testimony to the ingenuity of a people who somehow managed to provide a lot for their families out of very little. Now a new era was dawning, as I have related earlier, new and exciting foods to revolutionise our eating habits and to change our lives forever. For the better? I don't know.

At this particular time there had been a crisp revolution. Gone were the plain crisps with the little blue sachet of salt inside the packet. A sort of do it yourself system. The public demanded more variety for their four pence. New flavours were introduced: salt and vinegar, cheese and onion and many more.

Always looking for something new, I was introduced by a rep, a travelling salesman, to a brand new flavour of crisp. These crisps were delightfully called Hedgehog flavoured allegedly tasting of hedgehog. No one I knew had ever been in the close proximity of a hedgehog unless they had run over one in their car. The first and most important fact to ascertain was, were they kosher? If they weren't then the whole marketing ploy would be squashed flat. The ingredients were checked and there was nothing offensive for the authorities to get prickly about as the flavourings contained no naughties that could stop us from selling them.

It seemed too good an opportunity to miss, have a bit of fun and be the first kosher shop under the Manchester Beth Din to sell this new line. I therefore ordered a rather large quantity and duly placed an advert in the local paper, namely The Jewish Telegraph, with the heading Who Said That Hedgehogs Were Not Kosher?

The reaction was mixed. Most people thought that they tasted like nothing they had tasted before, which was presumably a correct assumption. The sales were reasonably steady and the crisps were bringing in new faces to try this new kosher phenomenon. I planned to sell them for maybe another week or two and then move on to some other offer and thought nothing more about it. A couple of uneventful days passed and on a particularly busy Tuesday we heard the screeching of tyres emitting from two Volvo estates blocking the entrance to the shop. Looking through the window I was amazed to see a minyan - that's at least ten rabbis dextrously jumping out of the cars whilst holding on to their hats. No mean feat. Curiosity overcame me. What on earth could they want, these men in black? What on earth could we have done wrong fully knowing that our religious authorities were always moving the goal posts? One day everything was fine and the next it was not. Always something different, it was as if they spent days debating what they could find wrong and whom they could harass and evidently it must have been my turn on that particular day.

A newly appointed Rabbi from the New World was the spokesman:

'We see you are selling a product that in itself has nothing offensive in its ingredients to be deemed as *treife* but in the name of kashrus we have decided,'…. (and all the assembled religious gathering nodded in agreement)…… 'that it is not in the spirit of our religion for one of our licensees to sell a non-kosher mammal, even if it was in the shape of a crisp. Alas, it could confuse certain of our people as to what they can or cannot eat. So we ask you to take these offending potato crisps off your shelves immediately.'

Not believing what I had just heard, I broke out in uncontrollable laughter whilst the assembled gathering stood in bewilderment at my antics. When I recovered I promised them that I would donate the rest of my hedgehogs to the Salvation Army, as there were presumably not many Jews there who could become sinners.

This proves that it isn't only the hedgehogs that have all the pricks.

Ad from the Jewish Telegraph, 7th July 1956

CHAPTER 19

Never Trust Your Husband...
With a Bird

Christmas time in the 1970s was a very busy time for all the local stores. It was a time of plenty for the small shopkeepers and the market traders. A time when hard work was rewarding, a time before the supermarkets and giant retail organisations had strangled the livings and entrepreneurial skills of the individual. A time before big brother knew what we were doing before we did ourselves.

Although it was certainly not a pseudo-religious time for us, one could not help getting caught up with the fervour of the holiday. It was an opportunity for a well-earned rest for the staff and for a couple of days I would look after the store, as the supermarkets and other shops were not open on the Boxing Day. It was always a relaxing day, work in the morning and my beloved Manchester City in the afternoon. Mind you, it was never easy to be relaxed watching City as I think the good Lord seemed always to have been in the red persuasion of Manchester. As far as City were concerned, they would have to wait for the miraculous to happen some thirty years later, when a different god brought City a miracle, but I digress.

At that time, as I have already explained, we were not allowed to sell raw meats as everything in the kosher world was departmentalised. Butchers were not allowed to sell delicatessen and delis were not allowed to sell raw meats and poultry. The London shops could not sell their products to Manchester and we were not allowed to export anything to London - not that anyone in London would want to buy any provincial manufactured products; far beneath any southerners to be tainted by northern food. At that time, life as the Londoners knew it ceased to exist north of Watford.

It was in the south that they had funny sounding names for the familiar products, like chriine instead of chrain and biigles instead of baigles. Everything had an 'i' in it instead of an 'a', so how anyone could do business between the North South divide, when they practically did not understand that they were eating the same food was beyond me. Even the Beth Dins were involved, not wanting to let an opposing authority on to their patch. Nothing religious, but down to the lowest common denominator dictating a large part of our religion for them: money and fees.

As seasons come and go Christmas was a good time. One of our firsts was selling cooked turkeys, as I have previously mentioned, we were not allowed to sell raw ones. This proved to be quite a hit with the good people of Manchester. Firstly, many people were working and did not have the time or the inclination to cook a big bird. Secondly it saved them a lot of unnecessary mess and worry with the hit and miss of home roasting. Many a local Jewish Mum had produced burnt offerings. After all the day was a family occasion to be enjoyed by all. That year we cooked over one hundred birds. It was hard work but no complaints. Problems yes, but complaints, no.

The one problem was not really our problem: a lady called Stella had given her husband strict instructions to collect the family dinner and she had provided us with special tape to wrap around the reinforced box which would allow the bird to be safely carried and delivered back home where the hungry family would await and then enjoy their well-earned and richly deserved turkey dinner.

The problem that particular evening was weather oriented. We had a Manchester smog, a real pea souper. Ralph's journey to Prestwich should have taken him about fifteen to twenty minutes but unfortunately he was stuck in a crawl in a fog, with no assistance, intervention or caution from his wife. The aroma and temptation were just too much for this hungry guy.

It all started by him making a small hole with a penknife in the side of the reinforced box but the tempting aroma that escaped from the little tear in the side of the box was too much and as he sat in the crawling foggy jam he managed to rip a little more from the side of the box exposing a juicy wing. No one would ever miss one turkey wing from such a large turkey, he must have thought and, as a very hungry man, he made an instant decision: he ripped the wing off and devoured it. The problem was that he had only driven a few hundred yards when he started poking a hole in the other side of the box where the other wing was matched and despatched with the same enthusiasm as its mate.

Another few hundred yards nearer home and first one leg closely followed by the other were devoured by a man on a mission. As he crossed Sheepfoot Lane on the Bury New Road one of the breasts had gone and now our turkey carrier, fearing that it may well have been his last supper and he may as well be hung for a sheep as well as a lamb, figuratively speaking, started on the second one. At this moment in time the smog miraculously lifted and dear Ralph found himself outside his driveway with a turkey carcass, a very greasy ripped strengthened cardboard box entwined with extra strong gaffer tape that had not stood a chance.

As he turned the van engine off he was greeted by wife and hungry children eagerly awaiting their roast turkey dinner. What happened next is anybody's guess, but I received a phone call from an angry and distraught wife pleading with me to help her out and bring her some food to feed the family. I duly drove back from south to north Manchester, opened the shop up and took whatever was left for Stella and family. That evening the S family celebrated the festival with a worsht and egg dinner. Ralph was subsequently banned from family shopping for ever.

Harry Hyman (my Dad) slicing smoked salmon.

CHAPTER 20

Smoke Gets in Your Eyes

S almon smoking was and is still an art and its end product, smoked salmon was certainly an expensive and privileged luxury in those days. Only the wealthier customers could afford to buy it. After all, the best smoked salmon was thirty shillings a pound - that was seven and six (7/6d) a quarter. We even sold it in two ounce lots at three and sevenpence halfpenny (3/7½d). People would vie for the smoke salmon skin. They would take it home and slice or scrape every last piece of salmon from it to make a sandwich.

This was the era before salmon farming gave this wonderful fish to all the people at sensible and affordable prices, although the farmed salmon could never match the quality and taste of the first spring fish of the year. As the fish came in from the sea and into the estuaries, they were in prime condition to start their long trek up the rivers to spawn. This was the time when we bought all our salmon stocks for the year.

We had four weeks to buy, to take the head and guts out, pack them individually in greaseproof paper, repack them back into boxes and take them to the cold storage, which was the Union Cold Stores in Miller Street, in Manchester. This expensive time of the year was when you needed an understanding bank manager.

We smoked our own fish in a traditional and old fashioned way. We made sure that this precious commodity was always, well nearly always, perfect. The salmon had to be gutted, split, deboned, washed and scrubbed. After this process the fish then had to be cured in a coarse salt for a certain length of time, depending on their size. The salt would then be washed off in running cold water. They would then be hung in an oven on poles after being strung and skewered. The skewers were to stop the fish from curling up during the smoking process.

All this was quite straight forward until it came to the actual smoking of the salmon. This is where the art and expertise came in. Now the original smoker was in fact a great big chimney that had been enlarged and lined with steel. A large metal frame on wheels held up to 30 sides of salmon. The oven had two steel doors and on the floor of the oven was a gas jet covered over with a steel sheet. The oak chippings were placed on the metal sheet. On top of the sawdust oak chippings was placed a small handful of saltpetre. We had to have a special licence for this product because beside it being used for pickling it was very combustible and was widely used for explosives. The great fun was lighting the saltpetre which, when it caught alight, was similar to letting off fireworks on bonfire night. The firework in question was called a snow storm and it made a very bright light and burned so hot for about ten seconds that it set the oak chippings alight and they started to smoulder, creating the smoke for the salmon, thus smoked salmon.

The problem was that the temperature for the smoking had to be just right. Too hot and you finished up with overcooked fish and impossible to slice, although it tasted good. Now some clever marketing guy, presumably after a gigantic over cooked cock up, came up with the name hot smoked and created a brand new product. Too cold and it finished up like modern day sushi, which way back in the fifties was definitely a no-no as who in their right mind at that time would eat raw fish? Therefore the temperature had to be just right. I am not allowed to divulge what the cooking temperature should be as it was a family secret passed down from Grandpa Joseph, of *Titanic* fame, to my Dad and then in a cloak of secrecy to me and I have now passed down this family heirloom to my son Richard.

In the summer the oven doors would have to be left open to let the heat out and in the winter partially closed to keep the heat in. Spring and autumn created their own problems but eventually it was possible to ascertain the correct temperature by sticking your hand in the oven and gauge by feel what the temperature should be. This was, believe it or not, ninety five percent accurate and the next morning there would be hanging thirty or so beautifully smoked fish, each with a fabulously healthy shiny sheen on them making for a mouth-watering gastronomic treat for all our customers.

It had to happen and it was inevitable that it would be at around three in the morning or thereabouts. Some inebriated bright spark, stumbling home from a pub, club or whatever, probably tanked up on Wife Beater, a well-known famous lager very popular with the locals. Staggered across Waterloo Road to the telephone kiosk opposite the shop and dialled 999. He told the operator that he could smell smoke coming from the premises over the road….. The one on the corner of Barrow Hill and Waterloo Road and would you summon the fire brigade urgently.

The fire brigade was brilliant. They arrived within five minutes, smashed the steel gates down at the rear of the property; they annihilated the back doors, chopping them into matchwood, raced into the factory areas and very diligently power hosed the smoke oven and the smoking salmon, causing a mini stream with bits of half smoked fish floating on it as if the salmon had gone full circle, were freed and were on the way home back to their river where they had been spawned.

When I arrived on the scene at about four o'clock, after having been summoned with an urgent telephone call that there had been a fire on our premises in Waterloo Road, it was with understandable fear and trepidation as to what and how had this thing happened. My first reaction on entering the building was as though a mini tsunami had hit the rear smoking area of the factory. Utter devastation.

A triumphant fireman informed me that they had saved the rest of the premises from destruction and were very pleased with their final result, as only the rear of the premises had been destroyed. He explained to me that unfortunately the greatest damage was always caused by the need for a quick entry and the water damage that the powerful hoses caused but they had had a good result and the danger had passed.

After a very long moment and when I finally composed myself, I explained to the chaps from the fire department that they had just drowned a lovely batch of Scottish partly smoked salmon. There had been no fire, which disproves the theory that there is no smoke without fire. Not only had they ruined my beautiful salmon and a night's sleep for me, they had managed to completely destroy the rear of my newly refurbished premises.

One could only imagine the comments from some of my customers and the local wags over the ensuing weeks regarding times of fires and insurance claims.

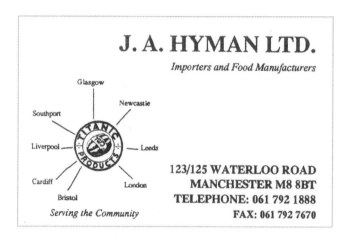

The Titanics business card.

CHAPTER 21

The Three Day Week

It's a funny old world. What's bad for most people is always good for a few, especially the opportunists.

In the 1970s there had been a great social upheaval. The unions were still trying to flex their muscles and look after the welfare of the workers and the government of the day was doing its best to modernise industry and wrest a great deal of power away from the unions. Who was right? It depended on which side of the political spectrum you were on.

The miners, with Jack Scargill at the helm, decided to take on the government and eventually called a strike, which created many a bloody confrontation with the police. It was the beginning of a dark period in the UK, both literally and metaphorically. Eventually, with the coal stocks rapidly diminishing causing the threat of power cuts, the politicians, in their wisdom, introduced an act of parliament stating that all businesses would only have electrical power for any three days out of five in a working week.

In the beginning this caused a considerable inconvenience to many a business but the British are resourceful and lots of people innovated with all sorts of devices and gadgets. The outdoor stores had a field day. Camping stoves, Tilly lamps and candles helped to oil the wheels of industry. Stoves fuelled with Esso Blue or Aladdin pink paraffin heated the offices and showrooms. Somehow businesses not only survived but most did as much business in three days as they had done in five, surprising but true.

There were exceptions to this three day week, grocery shops and food factories being some. I suppose the theory was keep the people well fed and avert a bloody revolution. We were amongst the fortunate few who were able to function for the full five days and were therefore exempt from a penal fine for non-compliance. This was fine for Dad but as a working teenager at the time, not so good as a two day holiday every week seemed to me to be a great idea.

The opportunities that arose with this three day week were enormous, especially for the entrepreneurs in our community. They scoured Europe for any form of lighting that was available at that time. Candles being the most practical and time proven form of lighting were the bounty hunters' way to that pot of gold that sometimes was at the end of their rainbow. This time it was the jackpot. It was so simple! Everyone was desperate for any kind of illumination and candles of every shape colour and size were brought into the country. It was indeed easy money. The first lots were bought and sold as soon as they appeared. Containers of candles were imported, landing in every available dock in the country. As soon as they were landed they were sold. After all, there were quite a few million people who had to have some form of lighting.

Unfortunately for the candle boys, greed had got the better of them. What they did not but should have realised is that nothing, no matter how lucrative, lasts for ever. They should have made their profit and moved on to something else. The lights were switched back on.

The wax market was swamped with candles of every hue and size. I was informed that if the wicks of all the extra candles that had been brought into this country over the past few weeks were tied together it would encircle the earth at least seven times. Whether anyone ever believed that was a matter of conjecture, but the country was awash with unwanted candles.

When Mrs. Cohen came in for her weekly shop she was greeted by hundreds of Sabbath candles recently purchased, of various sizes. All, if I may be so bold, bought and sold at a very reasonable price. After all, if the candles were good enough for the Vatican and all the

European cathedrals and churches they were good enough for Mrs. Cohen of Broughton Park to light on Friday night and bring in and bless the Sabbath.

Our Titanics logo.

CHAPTER 22

Dates and Degrees

In the late twentieth century, the 1980s if my memory serves me correctly, the government announced that that it was making it compulsory to date all food and soft drink products. The law was to ensure that people would see the clearly marked dates on the food and drink labels. If they were in date they would be fit to eat or drink. If they were not...?

Some of our older customers had told me that they had hoarded various tinned foods during the Second World War and they were still enjoying the contents some forty years on, with no ill effects and they had no dates on them. They did not know what all the fuss was about. One little old lady, Mrs. Levy, told me that she always checked her various foods to see if they were edible. Her rule of thumb being if they didn't have green things, as she put it, growing in or on the food and the tin wasn't blown it was fine to eat. She did confess that she tried the food first on her husband and if he suffered no ill effects then she would feed any guests and, of course, her beloved pet dog.

The government declared retailers would find it easier to rotate their stocks by just checking the dates, thus enabling the older products to be sold before the fresher ones. Simple. That's what the authorities reasoned but like all new regulations they had not worked out their new rules in practice but only in theory. Shop workers were needed to implement them and people being people, especially when shelf stacking, would always take the easy way out and put the fresh goods in front of the old, thus causing chaos and many mix ups. If only in their wisdom they would have sent out guidelines on how to implement the new rules and a little education for all, it would have been very useful.

The manufacturers themselves did not know how long their products would keep in a fit condition either. Everyone was in the dark and would have to learn by trial and error. Subsequently, in complete ignorance of the new system, they panicked and put a ridiculously short date on their products.

Two of the firms that we had business dealings with and bought a reasonable amount of their products bemoaned the fact that they had not quite understood the new dating system yet and they were stuck with a tremendous amount of stock that they had labelled with a six month shelf life...five months having already passed leaving only one month to distribute their products and for the retail shops to sell them on to their customers. They were stuck because no retail store would buy the goods as there would not be sufficient time to sell them before the expiry date.

Realising their predicament I offered to help them out and buy their entire stocks, at a price of course, without quibbling about the quantity or variety of the goods, as I reasoned that we had regularly sold these products. Some of them had been on the shelves for a lot longer than the six month date and there had never been a problem or complaint regarding their freshness.

One of the firms manufactured and supplied biscuits for the kosher and vegetarian market. All their biscuits were *parev*, which means that they were manufactured with no milk products and were made solely with vegetable oils. The religious people preferred biscuits that were parev, just in case any of their children had unknowingly eaten a biscuit containing a milk product and then had eaten a meat or chicken dinner. Never mix your *milchick* with your *fleishick.*

The other company supplied fruit juices in cartons both large and small. We were able to sell all of their products, with the exception of the grape juice that they produced. As grape juice was deemed not to be kosher and treated as if it was wine, which had to be supervised during its manufacture.

A couple of days later this giant truck arrived with a forty foot container in tow and the driver informed me that we were the proud owners of twenty palettes of fruit juice. Now for the uniformed there were fifty-five cases of large drinks and if my memory serves me correctly one hundred and ten small cases on each pallet. Making a total of approximately one thousand five hundred cases of assorted juices, about thirty thousand individual drinks. I had not put much thought into the quantity or how I would be able to sell them but a bargain was a bargain and a challenge was a challenge.

To make matters more exciting, as soon as the huge truck had been unloaded with all the drinks another very large lorry arrived with hundreds of cases of kosher biscuits. Thankfully it was a dry day as our forecourt was awash with biscuits and fruit juice. With a lot of local help the goods were stored away covering every nook and cranny in the building. The orthodox community do not and did not read the local or any papers but they have an amazing bush telegraph and word of any bargain goes round their community like wildfire. The religious people in the community, who in the main had large families, could not resist a bargain. I was once told by one of my Dad's friends, a butcher from

Altrincham, a lovely guy called Harold Willey, that if you had a shop in the jungle and you could supply goods that people wanted, they would hack their way through the undergrowth to find you. How right he was! Fruit juices and biscuits all selling for two pounds per case. Too good to be true! People came into the shop from all over Manchester and other religious communities who had never set foot in the shop before. It was a fascinating insight into the different religious sects and sections of our community.

The sad thing was, although we were the same religion and were under a high level of kashrus supervision, not only had I never set eyes on these people before but I never even knew that they existed, or lived in and around Manchester.

It was very colourful, with every group dressing differently in black. The men always seemed to be the ones who did the bargain shopping and were always accompanied by their children in tow behind them. The eldest and biggest near Dad and the smallest and youngest in the rear. It was like a brood of ducklings following the drake. One of our regular customers reckoned that it was like watching Ken Dodd and his Diddymen, as even the children wore large hats, very entertaining (Ken Dodd being the hit comedy show at that time).

I soon realised the reason why the entire family had been brought shopping. It was for porterage purposes, having large families needed large quantities of food and drinks. The children would each carry a box of juice or biscuits back to their old Volvo estate, Volvos being the religious car of choice at the time. Everyone was happy, they with the bargains and me with my new clientele, knowing full well that as soon as the bargains finished they too would disappear, like melting snow in warm sunshine. Loyalty to non-believers was certainly not their strong suit.

Unfortunately it did not take long for the companies producing the biscuits and drinks to realise that the dates appearing on their products were woefully inaccurate, the biscuits and drinks were fit for sale for twice as long as the dates that they had first guessed. We had been their guinea pigs.

The experience opened up other opportunities; I realised that everybody loves a bargain and there were plenty to be had about at that time. A new era in the history of JAH was about to begin.

One incident that I recall was the visit of the Pope to Manchester in 1982. He was to travel in his Popemobile through the streets of Prestwich and finish in Heaton Park, with an open air mass for all the Catholics in and around Manchester. The 'boys', that's the swag boys, reckoned that they would make a killing, not actually kill someone but make a lot of money, after all this was the first visit of the leader of the Catholic Church to Manchester. There would be thousands of people wanting to see and hear the Pope. All these good folk waiting for his arrival would surely want something to eat and drink to pass the time away. They would be lining the streets and would not want to move from their vantage points.

It was easy. The 'boys' would buy thousands of cases of soft drinks at a good price, mainly Coca Cola and whilst all these thousands of good Catholic people waited for their spiritual leader to pass surely they would become thirsty and want to buy the drinks, at a price. A captive audience, it would be a doddle, easy money. If I recall it was a warm and sunny day, as if ordered by some divine influence from above. The perfect day to stand by the roadside waiting to catch a glimpse of the Pope and to sell thousands of cans of soft drinks to the waiting masses.

What the 'boys' never realised was that the thousands of families waiting at the roadside were all good people. They had provided complete picnics for their children and themselves, knowing that there would be a long wait to see their Pontiff and were, therefore, completely self-sufficient. The thousands of cases of drinks were in the main superfluous to requirements. In fact the 'boys' had completely miscalculated their intended clientele and were lumbered.

The next day being Monday there was still a buzz of excitement in the air from the successful historical visit on Sunday. I was going about my dreary Monday morning duties when the telephone rang. I was called to the 'phone and the person on the other end of the line asked me if I was interested in buying a considerable quantity of Coca Cola and other soft drinks. Having seen what had happened, as we had spent the Sunday afternoon with our good friends Hilary and Edmund Rose who lived directly opposite Heaton Park, I knew that the soft drink sellers had had a bad selling day, judging by the mountains of cases of soft drinks still on the pavements long after the occasion was over.

The telephone was busy all day with people trying to sell cans of soft drinks and, indirectly through the good offices of his Holiness the Pope, the entire local Jewish community enjoyed months of bargain priced cans of fizzy drinks.

CHAPTER 23

Kicking the Weed

I started smoking at the tender age of eleven. The earliest recollection was buying five fags between three of us, and then democratically splitting the other two equally.

Everyone smoked. Every film star had a cig in his or her mouth or delicately poised between two fingers. Having brown nicotine stains on and between your fingers was a smoker's badge of honour. The cigarette brands all had exotic and exciting names.

Bill, who was the factory manager for Dad at that time, smoked the working man's cig, Woodbines, or sometimes Park Drive. Jennifer's Aunty Lily smoked Black Cat which presumably tasted like one. The middle class cigarette was called Embassy and they gave a voucher with every packet of their cigarettes. If you collected enough of these vouchers and smoked thousands of their cigarettes you could send away for a free gift ranging from a pen to an electric drill, providing one was still well enough to use them.

Mum and Dad were Players Medium devotees and it eventually began to affect my Mum's health and she gave up when she was ninety-one, having moved her brand on to Lambert and Butler. Jennifer, who considered herself as Miss Chic smoked Passing Cloud or, when really trying to impress, Black Russian.

I, having graduated from Players Weights, moved up the social smokers ladder progressing from Senior Service, then moving on to the safer Rothmans filter cigarettes and finally settling on Silk Cut. I smoked anywhere and everywhere, from first thing in the morning, after cleaning my teeth, with my cup of tea, on the way to work in the car and, of course, at work. Which looking back in time is astonishing as we had a food store, but everyone smoked.

I even recall Mr Tanner, who had served in the RAF with my Dad in India during the second world war and was now a food and hygiene inspector for the Environmental Health, used to inspect the premises with the proverbial fine toothed comb and was very exacting as to what the standards should attain, always had a cigarette in his mouth.

I recall my Aunty Lilly, the one with the blue rinse, being asked by the customers not to drop ash on their smoked salmon as she was hand slicing it with a cigarette in her mouth. Nevertheless, they came back week after week for the same smoked salmon, never considering that anything was amiss.

I was a little more subtle in my approach to the fag hanging in mouth situation. I always put my cigarette down either on the side of the till, that is the cash register, or on the edge of a counter whilst serving my customer, thus causing hundreds of scorch marks and burns, making a novel pattern along the edges.

This went on for years and then in the late 1970s we were told that maybe smoking was not so cool after all and it definitely was not conducive to healthy living. My Dad was just recovering from a nasty heart attack, which we were told was mainly due to years of heavy smoking. This had given me a nasty shock and, as I was thirty-seven and although I felt fine, I began to think that I was pushing my luck.

My body was virginal metaphorically speaking. I had never done any proper exercise; even at school I wagged as much as I could. In those days it was not the done thing to wear long trousers until one attained the age of thirteen, post Bar Mitzvah. I remember in my first year at Stand Grammar school one particularly cold winters day handing the gym, now known as PE, teacher a letter from my Mum explaining to him that it was too cold for her little boy to participate in cross country running as it made his little legs very sore and chapped. As one can imagine this did not go down very well with Mr. Hargreaves, our PE teacher.

Cross country or any other form of exercise was like purgatory to me and I was told by some wiser kids to run with enthusiasm until out of sight, hide and wait for everyone to return and then latch on to the back of returning runners and pretend that you had completed the course and would then avoid punishment from the very scary Mr Hargreaves. On reflection I don't think that I fooled our teacher for one moment, but he had given me up as a lost cause.

I now realised that I had to do something to stop the slide down the slippery slope and finish up an even bigger slob than I was becoming. The first and most important issue was to stop smoking. Saying it seemed easy but turned out to be one of the most difficult things that I have achieved in my entire lifetime to date.

I spoke to Ronnie about the possibility of stopping smoking, and we both realised that we were junkies, hooked on nicotine, tar and crap, not to mention the fumes of industrial Manchester that were entering our lungs and that would eventually adversely affect our health. Ronnie's cousin had heard of a clinic in Chorlton, a suburb of Manchester that specialised in helping people to stop smoking. This clinic was run by a Dr. Chris Steele, who had a unique method of helping people who were hooked on the tobacco weed. I telephoned the clinic for an appointment. A date duly made, Ronnie and I went in trepidation to see what was involved for this miracle cure.

Firstly we were told you had to want to stop smoking, which was logical enough. As we said that after smoking heavily say thirty cigarettes a day for nearly thirty years some three hundred thousand each, a scary statistic, enough was more than enough. I had decided that I wanted to become physically fit, as I had never had the fun of playing competitive games and I had dreams of becoming an athlete and eventually running a marathon.

We duly went to the clinic, which was in Chorlton cum Hardy, and were introduced to Dr. Steele who explained the difficult path that we would have to go down to stop smoking. We were given a sealed envelope with instructions to be opened at home and told to report back to the clinic in three weeks' time for the final sessions of this very new and novel therapy. Little did I realise what was in store for me.

The instructions were very simple and easy to follow. For the next twenty days all I had to do was to write down the enjoyment factor of each cigarette smoked, five being the most enjoyable and satisfying and one the least. Easy enough.

For the next twenty days I duly noted this enjoyment and satisfaction factor of every fag. The amazing statistic that emerged from this exercise was that of all the cigs I had smoked over the last three weeks only two had received a five whilst most had a one or two rating, proving that most of the cigarettes that I smoked were through habit and were definitely not for enjoyment. The sting in the tail was that on the last day and twenty-four hours before going back to the clinic for the final test I had to smoke twice the number of cigarettes that I normally smoked on an average day.

Some sixty cigarettes were smoked on the twenty-first day. Not feeling so good, for obvious reasons, I took myself off to the clinic and met my mate Ronnie, who looked as sick and worried as I did as he had also doubled his normal intake of cigarettes on this particular and hopefully momentous day.

We sat in the waiting room and after an anxious ten minutes were called and briefed at the same time as to what fate awaited us next. A very attractive nurse asked us to follow her to a room full of cubicles, a little like where one would vote, or the booths one goes to take their own photograph. These cubicles had a curtain around them and all that I could smell was the strong aroma of cigarette smoke wafting above the curtains and filling the room with acrid tobacco fumes.

On entering the cubicle I noticed that there was a mirror and on either side of this mirror were two ashtrays full of smouldering cig ends. I was presented with two Capstan full strength cigarettes, one for each hand, and told to look into the mirror whilst puffing on first one of these extra strong cigarettes and then the other.

It did not take long before I felt physically sick, besides looking at myself in the mirror with a lit cig in either hand. I had been doubly tanked up on nicotine over the past twenty-four hours and was praying that they would let me out of this curtained prison. Thankfully, just as I was about to either throw up or pass out, I was rescued by the nurse, led out of the smoke den and told to rest for a while before being given my instructions as to what I could and could not do over the next twenty four hours.

When Ronnie emerged he also looked worse for wear, maybe a tad greener than me but nevertheless still able to walk. We had completed the next stage in the process.

Our instructions were simple. No smoking for the next twenty-four hours, return to the clinic the next day where we would be permitted to smoke under supervision. Even as a hardened smoker I had certainly had enough smokes for one day and I managed to drive myself home and explained what had happened to me in gory detail to Jennifer. I had a cup of tea and went straight to bed.

I awoke in the morning not being sure if I wanted a cigarette or not and managed to get through a surreal day, almost as if in a trance. It was difficult not smoking but I had come this far so I reckoned that I could manage for a few more hours until I returned to the clinic where at least I would be able to have a smoke.

I arrived at the clinic at my allotted appointment time and was confronted by a greenish coloured apparition.

'Ronnie,' I said, 'you look awful!'

'Thanks…' was the reply. 'You don't look so good yourself.' And he was correct. I felt awful.

We were ushered into the same torture cubicles as the previous night and went through the same ritual as we had twenty-four hours ago with the two full strength cigarettes. Clouds of cigarette smoke filling and polluting the atmosphere. It definitely was not fun and as I puffed and inhaled on each cig I felt more and more dizzy and nauseous. I was just about to shout the nurse and tell her that I had had enough aversion therapy for that night when I heard a groan and the crash of a falling body.

I quickly exited from the smoke den to witness my pal Ronnie being given oxygen by one of the nurses. He had succumbed to an overdose of smoke, nicotine and tar. Thankfully he recovered quickly and after a rest was allowed to drive himself home. Thirty years on and he still denies passing out on that particular night but how could he remember when he was unconscious at the time? The same procedure as the night before. No smoking until the third and final visit to the now hated clinic. The same cubicles and the same lit cigarettes and the same terrible fumes of concentrated tobacco smoke and then it was over, finished, cured, never wanting to smoke again. How wrong I was. I was told that they had played their part and now it was up to me to finally kill this habit. The next twenty-eight days would be crucial. What I did not realise at the time was that I was a drug addict. Hooked on nicotine. Nevertheless I went home happy with the knowledge that I did not ever have to return to that clinic in Chorlton again and apprehensive in the way that I would cope without the help of a cigarette.

My memories of the next twenty-eight days are vague. I just about managed to exist. I felt dizzy, irritable, hot and cold. My craving for a cigarette was tempered by the nauseous thoughts of my recent smoking aversion therapy treatment and the hope that soon my cravings would subside and life would normalise once again.

I wondered why Jennifer went out to her sister Lisa's house every night when I returned from work. It was only years later that she told me that every time she saw me she had a craving to smoke a cigarette. I thought that if I had gone instead to a brothel would it have had the same result. I had begun to think that she had an aversion to me as she always gave me a reasonable excuse for going down the road and at the time I was definitely not functioning correctly and never realised the purpose of those visits. I'm pleased that she didn't tell me at the time. It proves how powerful the impact of this drug is, not only on the smoker but also on those around.

Four weeks later I was feeling a little less like a zombie. Although my constant thoughts were still tobacco related, I had been advised that every time I had the urge to smoke, I should eat a piece of chocolate. Even if I put weight on it would be easier to go on a diet to lose the added weight than to try and stop smoking again.

Each passing month the urge to smoke eased and I began to try and get fit. I had always dreamt of being a runner and I started jogging, at first half a mile and then a half marathon and eventually running a full marathon with my running partner Laurence Cohen, a lovely guy, full of fun, although misguided in his support of the soccer team on the darker side of Manchester. This led on to other stupendous events in my life.

Stopping smoking was down to a determination to move on in my life and enjoy all the activities that I had only dreamt about. I have not smoked a cigarette since my final visit to that clinic some thirty years ago. My eternal thanks go to Dr. Chris Steel for giving me the chance to rediscover the good and fun times in my life.

CHAPTER 24

Charlie Lands Me in a Pickle

I remember it was a June day, nothing much was happening. Everyone was running down their stocks in fridges and freezers in anticipation of the summer holidays. The barbecue season was again a non-starter, typical Manchester weather. Passover was long gone and our world seemed in limbo. If only someone, anyone would telephone, or call with a good bargain to brighten up the day. And then:

'There are some guys in the shop who want to know if you are interested in buying some pickled cucumbers?' I was informed. '....Are you interested?'

'Maybe.'

Nothing better to do I wander nonchalantly into the shop where I see Raymond, an old acquaintance from a past era sometime long ago in my youth. Raymond, I remembered went to Laps. That is, Lapidus Chip Shop, where everyone in their early teens met on a weekend evening. Now I always remember Raymond because he was the only one of us who could afford a hot salt beef sandwich, with mustard and sweet and sour cucumber whilst we could only afford chips. I was always envious of this guy. Mind you I should not have been, his only attribute being the product of lucky sperm.

Alongside Raymond was some gentleman from Liverpool whom Raymond had met whilst on a holiday sponsored by the Queen. The introductions were very cordial, especially as Raymond's friend was big, very big. Although it was nice to renew old acquaintances they soon got down to business. Was I interested in buying a job lot of pickled cucumbers? Of course I was, I would buy virtually anything if it was cheap enough and, of course, kosher. That is, in both interpretations of the word. Raymond's friend went to the van parked on the forecourt. It seemed to be carrying a very heavy load and it was so weighed down that it seemed on the verge of collapse. He returned with a jar of Dutch cucumbers without a label. I knew that they were from the Netherlands because they had a number on the bottom of the jar which depicted the country of origin. So far so good. The jar was opened and passed around the staff who were all experts on pickles for comments. All seemed okay. The question was then raised as to why Raymond and colleague had such an odd job lot. The rather large gentleman from Merseyside told me that it was a consignment which had originally been destined for a supermarket but had been refused because of late delivery and it was well known that I would have a go, so they had come to see me.

The next question was how many jars, because it was difficult to guess, as they were all loose in the back of this van. The Scouse gentleman shrugged and asked me if I wanted to buy them to make an offer. I had not a clue but judging by the weight on the van there were a lot. I offered £200 and this was immediately accepted. Then I realised that I had paid too much but my word being my bond I went to write out a cheque. This was accepted although they may have expected cash but I did not do readies and wanted a receipt. The van was unloaded and I reviewed my purchase, the shop being full of pickled cucumbers. Not bad for a quiet June day. We could sell them at two for a pound, which was virtually half price. I went home that night happy.

A few days later Raymond's friend turned up at the door again. Would I be interested in buying another van load of these cucumbers? This time I offered £100 and to my surprise and amazement the offer was accepted. Maybe I had still paid too much but what the hell, they were cheap enough. The problem was, where could we store them all? There were so many jars of cucumbers in the shop that it was difficult for the customers to move around but they always accepted that there was always something unusual happening, and they seemed to enjoy the chaos. That was what JAH was, zany and fun. It would lighten an ordinary humdrum day.

A week later he was back, that is the minder. Did I want any more cucs? Sure enough, the van was there still loaded full of jars of pickled cucumbers. This time I asked if there were any more in their store, and was told there was another van load. I did not want any more but I told him I would give him £50 for the total lot of the two loads. To my amazement he accepted and we were cucumbered out from floor to ceiling, but a bargain was a bargain. I wondered why they were so cheap but life throws up strange situations and more.

I move on. We are now in October and I receive a phone call from Charles Bloom who, besides being a very good friend, was an eminent barrister who some years later became a judge. He was defending some guy from Liverpool who had been accused of smuggling a large quantity of cannabis into the country from Holland. These drugs, the prosecution stated, had been brought into the country, secreted among pallets of pickled cucumbers, sweet and sour no less, everyone's favourite. The defence said that they bought a job lot of cucumbers and had no knowledge of the existence of twenty-five kilos of cannabis.

This is where I became involved, as the defendant told the court that he had sold the entire consignment to some little fat fellow in Manchester, but could not remember his name but the store was somewhere in the North of the city.

Charles being very astute deduced that it could only be one person who would buy such a package. Sure enough, I received a 'phone call from him and, after verifying that I was indeed that very person, he asked me if I would go to Knutsford Crown Court on Thursday next as a witness for the defence. I reluctantly agreed.

The following Monday lunchtime I was telephoned by Charles stating that the defendant had indeed sold me the cucumbers and had been paid in readies (cash) and that the Inland Revenue was at the court and wanted to question me as to why I had paid cash and not cheque and they were coming to Manchester to do a visit. I tried to tell Charles that I had given cheques for my pickles and not cash but he just sighed and said, 'Sorry but be prepared.' A bad hour ensued because nobody wants visits like this, innocent or not.

About an hour later another call from my barrister friend telling me that he had been winding me up because I had thrashed him at tennis a couple of days earlier. He always was a crap player. It is very funny now but I had had a very bad hour.

Now Thursday was a very busy day and it was a great sacrifice to leave work to go and sit in a courtroom, waiting to be called as a witness for some case that I had not the slightest interest in the outcome. I sat all day and was not called. As I was leaving Charles said,

'Sorry but will see you in the morning, don't be late. We will try and have you on the witness stand first so you will be able to go back to work.'

I duly arrived in the morning and felt very apprehensive as I had never been a witness and had never stood in the witness box.

I was duly called upon and as I recall, the questioning from Charles went as follows:

'Is your name Stanley Hyman?'

'YES.'

'And is your shop called J.A.Hyman or Titanics?'

'YES.'

'And was your grandfather a survivor from the *Titanic* disaster?'

'YES.'

'Do you smoke your own exquisite salmon which we buy all the time?'

'YES.'

'And do you have a wonderful range of both raw and cooked meats?'

'YES.'

At this moment the judge interjected and asked if this was relevant to this case. Charles told the judge that it was not, but as I had given up two days of my time, I was entitled to a little free publicity. Everyone thought that this was hilarious except the judge. After ten minutes of questioning I was allowed to leave and go back to work. A week or so later I was told that my witnessing had been in vain and the cucumber salesman was convicted of drug smuggling and was sent down for a number of years.

A couple of years later we went to Eastbourne to see our old neighbours and good friends the Richs, who years earlier had escaped from the rat race of Manchester for the more gentle pace of the South Coast. Indeed, as I write he has just become the Zimmer frame champion of Eastbourne. GOOD ON YOU MIKE. Have to shout, it's like that down there. I believe that they get up in the morning and look at the obituary column in the local paper and if their name is not in it they go back to bed. Only joking.

One morning, after one of Gillian's special breakfasts (Gillian was a teacher and is extraordinarily well organised - you have to be well behaved or you get put on the naughty step), we were whisked away in the family

Prius. The very height of chic, in fact known as the Ferrari of Eastbourne, to watch the power boat racing in the harbour. The Customs and Excise were exhibiting on a stand to demonstrate their prowess at catching cunning smugglers and you would never guess, but our very own cucumbers were featured, demonstrating devious ways in which people imported drugs. When I told the customs officer that they were my cucumbers he did not seem to be impressed and was singularly underwhelmed, but it made a few pounds and a very good story.

CHAPTER 25

Me and the O'Learys

In 1992 I purchased a plot of land opposite our shop on Waterloo Road, which was called the Nordel site. This had been a smoked salmon and herring pickling factory from 1930-1950, named Northern Delicacies, hence the name Nordel. It was then acquired by various car dealers, the most famous being Syd Abrams, who had used the site as a commercial servicing area and also a new car storage depot. Abrams sold the business to a car storage firm as the yard was perfect for the job, being well protected from the local residents with a twenty foot high fence surrounding it.

We were struggling for storage space in our premises and I thought that I may be able to rent some space from the current owners of the yard. I met up with one of the partners, who told me that there had been a massive fallout and, as the senior partner, he wanted to sell and told me to name a price, which I did. To my amazement he accepted, on the understanding we completed within seven days to further annoy his partner. That was not my problem and that was how I acquired the yard at 170 Waterloo Road which included Ron, the car valeter.

For the first few months everything was going great. Ron had contracts with the local garages for cleaning and making good the new and used cars and we stored the new cars for the garages, as they had little space. All this was very lucrative. Alas easy money does not last forever. After a few months Ron the car valeter threw a wobbler and disappeared. I never knew what happened to him. He was there on a Friday and had vanished on the Monday. His rent being up to date, his mate Bob, who had occasionally helped, decided to carry on the car cleaning business.

For the first couple of weeks everything seemed fine. And then Bob was cleaning the engine of a brand new Peugeot, with its engine running, when into the yard run two local lads. They jump in to the running car and in an instant the boys and car have gone, last seen speeding down Waterloo Road with Bob looking on in disbelief.

No point in ringing the police, judges Bob, so he telephones the local enforcers for assistance. Five minutes later it all kicked off with all my staff watching as four huge Volvos screeched to a halt at the yard. Out jumps this giant of a man and, after consulting with the hapless Bob, bellows orders to all his men to find that car.

Two minutes later another Volvo turns up. The huge guy screams at the unfortunate driver something like, 'WHERE THE F*** HAVE YOU BEEN??' The guy stammers that he had gone to Waterloo Street by mistake, a small misjudgement you may reason, but it did not save the poor guy from a punch from the big man which knocked him flat.

'Next time effingwell listen!' he told the poor horizontal guy. We all looked on in disbelief.

Hello Patrick O'Leary!

Big Pat barked out orders to his men, they all shot off in different directions and believe it or not some thirty minutes later a new Peugeot with two very frightened local car thieves escorted by two Volvos, one behind and one at the front arrived back in the yard. Bob was a very relieved man, he had the car back and the garage would be none the wiser. This was great except for one very minor point, the guys very reasonably wanted paying for their very quick efficient and clinical work. Alas poor Bob had not thought of that. Oh, by the way, the two car thieves were very gently and thoughtfully taken to the local hospital where they were carefully placed in casualty. They would not be knocking off cars again for a very long time.

The next morning I went to work wondering what had been the outcome of the previous day's incident. I did not have long to wait. I apprehensively crossed over the road went into the yard and was greeted by this unfamiliar face. I enquired after Bob and to my amazement and disbelief the gentleman informed me that Bob the Knob was no longer working in this business because of the unpaid debt and that he, Duncan, had taken over.

'I'm your new tenant' said Duncan. I noticed the four rather large gold rings on Duncan's right hand. He told me that the rings had the first four letters of his name embossed on them: DUNC and were his calling card, so to speak, metaphorically.

'Very sensible' I told him, '…it saves buying business cards…' He did not seem impressed.

He then informed me that he would pay the same rent as the hapless Bob the Knob. I thanked him for this and enquired if he would set up a standing order with his bank; it would save me asking for the rent every week, and he may be too busy to remember. I received The Look and was told it would be in readies as he didn't do banks. I sensibly declined to comment and thanked him in anticipation. I then wished him well in his new career in car valeting and waited.

Everything went well for the first couple of weeks, and then the news spread like wildfire of what had happened and who was running the yard. Overnight the cars were all collected by the garages and when I came into work one morning there were no more cars in the yard to clean.

Duncan seemed a lot less perturbed than me. He told me that having no cars to clean meant that basically he could stay in bed in the morning for an extra couple of hours and then that would give him the energy to drink in the pub until late. He also told me that no work meant no rent but not to worry as I didn't really need it. Very kind and thoughtful of him telling me. That really was considerate.

As the weeks went by there seemed to be an impasse, me asking and he, when he turned up, shrugging that he was trying to find work. When I enquired, delicately of course, if maybe he would like to amicably give up his tenancy he told me that he was in a meaningful vocation and that it would be a sacrilege to stop. In other words 'F*** off! You must be joking mate!' Not wanting to have a permanent DUNC forcibly embossed on any part of my person, I backed off.

The weeks turned into months and nothing was happening. No work for them and no rent for me, a total stalemate and with these guys it was literally impossible to ask them to leave if you valued life. I racked my brain for weeks trying to fathom out some amicable solution that would get them out of the yard so life could continue as before and I would be able to find another tenant.

Then one morning the solution dawned on me. It was so simple why had I had months of sleepless nights? My Dad had been very friendly with a lot of the Italian lads who were brought up in New Cross, an area off Rochdale Road in Ancoats. They had all teamed up to fight against the Fascist Blackshirts in the 1930s and I had heard that Duncan and family were of Italian Irish descent. I was not sure if it was true or not but it would be worth a punt, so to speak and I was becoming desperate. A plan of action was hatching, a plan of pure chutzpah.

The following Tuesday, Tuesday being the optimum day, as the drinking habits of the locals dictated this: Friday, Saturday and Sunday were all drinking days and Mondays, as they used to say, were Salford holidays, a day for recovery, so as to be fresh and fit to start drinking and to be able to stagger to the next Friday where the cycle would recommence.

At about ten in the morning I saw my tenant DUNC and related to him my exciting discovery, I asked him the name of his granddad and when he told me his name I gasped in total astonishment. The very name my Dad had mentioned to me when he used to reminisce about the old days. What an amazing coincidence. I then asked if he was still alive but he told me alas he had passed away. This was a shame as I said that I would have liked to meet him to talk about the old days.

This startling revelation had a profound effect on Mr Duncan who immediately shook my hand and told me to hang around as he would return with some of his family.

I definitely was going nowhere and sure enough a couple of hours later a large number of the family appeared. They all came up to me, shook my hand and told me that any friend or offspring of their granddad had to have total respect and that they would be moving on to start another business elsewhere.

I immediately offered them a considerable amount of money for their entire stock which I have still in my possession to this day: the very wash leather, container of soap and bucket which I had paid some £500 for. A real bargain! They told me that I would never have any trouble with the locals and to this day they have kept their word.

Ad from Jewish Telegraph 29th September 1997.

CHAPTER 26

Mugging the Muggers

It is said that most of the population will be mugged at least once in their lives and I read in a newspaper recently that the younger generation accept this awful fact and are resigned that one day it will happen to them.

I had to be different because it happened to me twice. Both times on a Thursday at the same place, the former funny and scary, the latter very scary and yet funny.

In the 1970s it was the fashion for men to have handbags and my devoted wife bought me a fine leather handbag which was really not my scene as I always considered men with purses, handbags and wallets to be slightly effeminate and that real men stuffed hankies, keys, money and any other necessities into their trouser pockets just as they had done in their schooldays, when it was cigarette cards, marbles and catapult - as was the case with my handbag. In fact, it was like a grown up legacy from my primary school days. It was filled with old notes, not bank ones, but reminders of past meetings, business cards collected over the years, elastic bands, always useful. In fact it was full of junk. The only useful items stored in this tatty leather bag were my shop keys.

It was nearly six in the evening, everyone had said their good nights and had rapidly disappeared back into their own worlds. I set the alarm and locked the door, sighed contentedly, another day without major incident, meandered to my car, unlocked it and was just about to get inside when someone, from it seemed nowhere, jumped onto my back. My first reaction was that it was Mendel Feingold larking about. Why I thought it could be him I hadn't a clue but he worked nearby and was always around, looking for food as his lovely wife tried in vain to keep him on a strict diet. I had been sworn to secrecy regarding his dietary indiscretions. We had a deal, he prayed for me, as he was the cantor of the Whitefield synagogue and had a wonderful melodious voice and I fed him. I reckoned it worked as we were both content with our lots in life, me spiritually and him physically.

Unfortunately it was not. Before I was able to react this thug, whose appearance was nothing like Mendel's, threw a punch in my direction then pushed me up against the car, grabbed my handbag and ran off down Waterloo Road. As in all these incidents there was never anyone around, a policeman was a rarity in Hightown in those days so there was going to be no help there. So Stan, you were on your own.

What this hooded gentleman did not know as he legged it down Waterloo Road clutching my bag, was that the previous week I had run the Piccadilly Radio Manchester Marathon along with a good friend of mine Laurence Cohen – as I mentioned earlier - who made lampposts for a living. It was a good chat up line for the girls and he had just received an award from the Queen's corgis for his contribution for the welfare of dogs. And we were both reasonably fit.

By the time I had cleared my head, sorted myself out and realised that I had been attacked, my thief was two hundred yards away running it as fast as he could. I decided to follow him as I wanted all my shop keys back for obvious reasons and was hopeful that I would see a custodian of the law during my pursuit and be able to reclaim my belongings.

The guy reached the bottom of Waterloo Road, stopped, turned round and expected that he had got away with his attack and was now able to open the bag at his leisure and see what he had nicked. To his surprise he saw me in hot pursuit. He started running again across Bury New Road into Broughton Lane and onto Great Clewes Street. To his dismay I was only a few yards behind him and now he was very much out of breath and looking noticeably knackered.

He started running again but now a lot slower as he was on the point of exhaustion. After a couple of hundred yards more he finally stopped, completely shattered, picked up a brick and threatened to hit me with it if I came any nearer to him. I promised him that I valued my good looks and that I would not go any nearer to him but that I had just run a marathon and that I would follow him at a distance, of course, not wanting his brick or anything else on my head until we either found a copper, help or he dropped with exhaustion. My attacker by now was completely confused as he had never come across a situation like this one and was at a complete loss as to what he should do next.

We were now almost buddies or at least becoming acquaintances by this time and I offered to help him out of this, his most perplexing situation. I told him he could keep the bag with all its contents but I wanted the keys. He should throw them to me and I promised him that I would not follow him anymore and he could then enjoy all the other contents of the bag at his leisure. He seemed relieved at this suggestion and he asked me to promise not to tell anyone that he had negotiated with a victim as he would lose all his street cred with the local villains. I agreed, greatly amused that I had successfully outwitted a mugger. He then threw me my keys, which I thankfully picked up and then jogged contentedly back to my car.

My mugger had definitely not had a good day, besides being run to exhaustion he had stolen a load of rubbish which saved me chucking its contents away. I never used a handbag again.

My next unfortunate mugging experience was very scary. The first time I had been attacked it had turned out to be something of a lark. This time it certainly was not.

We were going through a purple patch at work, the marketing and advertising were paying off, I had always maintained that we were a community store and the community were showing their appreciation and were supporting us.

It was a sort of mutual admiration thing and we were extremely busy, especially on a Thursday, the best day of the week where the customers would buy the meat, poultry, and delicatessen for the coming weekend. One of my staff, whilst in the pub one evening and after one or two drinks, had evidently started bragging how busy we were at work and had presumably been overheard by some of the rougher elements of our criminal society. Completely unaware of any sinister plot being drawn up life carried on, until that fateful Thursday.

It had been another good day and 'see yers' having been said, everyone shot off home with the exception of Dorothy and me to lock up as usual. Shutters locked Dorothy went to the van and me to my car. I sat in the car and what happened next was akin to a horror movie. Suddenly a car screeched onto the forecourt and three guys with balaclavas covering their faces, wielding machetes surrounded my car & opened the driver's door. One of them stuck a machete onto my throat demanding the takings. I was unable to speak for two reasons. The first because of this sword being pressed onto my windpipe and the second was that I was terrified. My life seemed to flash by me, an old cliché but true and for the first time I realised that it was not my choice if I lived or not but some low life scum who would make this decision. It certainly did not feel good and what made it worse was that I could not see his face.

As all this was happening one of his accomplices went to the passenger door and triumphantly shouted GOT IT. Thankfully at this point the guy with the machete decided not to end my life, removed the machete from my throat, shouted in triumph and rushed back to the waiting getaway car along with his mates and of course the bag dropped in the well of the passenger seat; the days takings! The car screeched off the forecourt and I immediately awoke from this frightening scenario. I was in some state of shock and didn't know what to do next. Luckily Dorothy was still around and had witnessed the whole horror show but it had all happened so quickly that she had had no time to react and even if she had there would have been nothing that she could have done, seeing a machete stuck in her bosses throat and it being payday tomorrow no boss no pay. We then opened up the shop again and telephoned the police.

This was the era just before mobile phones. The police were relatively speedy that night. It only took them twenty minutes to arrive and they took off in their little panda car in the general direction of the thieves who had, by the way, some powerful looking BMW. After another thirty minutes I was told that this very car had been abandoned and set on fire. The thieves had stolen two cars and switched to the second one and had gone back to their hideout, presumably somewhere in lower Salford to share out the booty in their own time, planning between them what to do with the spoils. Quite an operation but they must have thought it worthwhile. Probably weeks of planning, stealing two cars, three big guys with masks, machetes and the will not to work at anything meaningful. Just thugs and bullies set upon one person who had just completed a hard day's work, with the sole idea of getting something for nothing and to hell with the anguish and fear that they would cause.

Meanwhile, after giving my statement to the police, and by the way I am still waiting for a reply some thirty years later, I assume that they never caught them or even cared. I suppose that in their eyes it was not a big deal but it was and still is to me.

I can only imagine what happened next in the sanctuary of their lair; the day's takings ready to be split three ways. It would keep them in booze, clothes or whatever for a few weeks until it was time to make more misery for some other poor unfortunate. They must have opened the carrier bag and tipped the contents with eager anticipation presumably onto a table ready to count the booty. Unfortunately for them they had violently stolen my supper and out of the bag tumbled a pair of kippers, two pieces of chopped and fried fish and a jar of chrain (horseradish and beetroot sauce), very tasty with chopped and fried. I would have loved to have been a fly on the wall at that particular moment to see their faces. I wonder if they enjoyed my supper.

Everyone later thought that this was hilarious, attacking someone, burning out two stolen cars just for their supper. The joke that went round afterwards at work was that if anyone brought back a jar of Simons Chrain and wanted to swap it for a jar of Elswood they had to notify the police immediately. By the way, the days takings were in my pocket. Very funny now but not at the time. A lesson learnt. Securicor collected all monies to the bank and back after that sour and sweet episode.

CHAPTER 27

The Shrinking Meat Balls and Other Amazing Phenomena

My Dad had always told me that trying to work with the kosher butchers of Manchester was, to say the least tricky, or very tricky, or very, very tricky.

They were, he said, always up to mischief of some kind or another. Which brings me to the story of Chaim Grease and some of his irregular, although highly successful business dealings.

There were only a limited number of customers for all the butchers to fight for, as basically we were only allowed to supply the good people of Manchester North and South and, of course, Salford. This was instigated by all the Beth Dins, the religious governing bodies so as to protect their income and stop any other religious body or town from straying on their patch, or vice versa. So if one butcher gained a new customer, it was that butcher's gain and it was another one's loss. It really was a cutthroat business, in more ways than one.

Chaim, who was very clever and cunning to say the least, had worked out a way of supplying the major local institutions in such a way that it was virtually impossible to undercut him. This, I later found out was his secret. He would sell them a whole side of beef, not the cuts. A side of beef for example weighing 100 lbs. in old money, (about 45 kilos), would cost £100 therefore quite logically the cost would be £1 per pound. Chaim would then add on some twenty percent for his overheads making the side of beef £120. He made £20 and this was, he said, for the labour, as it was unfair to profiteer. These were charitable institutions after all and one had to perform one's public duty. This all seemed to be very generous and kind as the competition could not come anywhere near to his costing being at least twenty percent more.

What he omitted to tell the customers was that when the side of beef was boned, porged and koshered, the bits left which he sold to the institutions only weighed about half the original weight. With around thirty percent being bones, what could have happened to the other twenty-odd percent you may wonder? The trouble was no one ever bothered to find out. It's amazing what the odd bottle of whisky could achieve. The bits and pieces were used as mince but here was another inspired move. Every load of meat destined for mincemeat was subject to a ritual of a bucket of water with red colouring. This really gave the mince a vibrant & healthy hue and of course a lot of extra weight.

The problem being that when the mincemeat was made into big mouth-watering meatballs and then cooked, the final product was not a big gezunte (tasty) meatball but pebble sized balls as the copious amounts of water evaporated in the cooking. Some of the elderly residents complained that they were unable to chew through these marble sized balls.

It is said that one enterprising resident asked for cocktail sticks so that he could suck his meatball like a lolly, as his new teeth couldn't chew through them. Another wanted to play marbles with them as he was quoted as saying that the marbles reminded him of his youth and he had not had this much fun for years but could they use less gravy as they were sticking to the carpet.

When confronted Chaim blamed the BD supervisor for koshering the meat with too much water. I knew about too much salt but not too much water and he always got away with it! The institutions never knew how big a rib, the best cut, or the bola or brisket really was and our friend Chaim wasn't going to tell, as presumably the cuts were sold in his butchers shop for a very good price.

The saying goes that you can kid some of the people all of the time and all of the people some of the time but our Chaim managed all of the people all of the time. Maybe it wasn't only the meatballs that were greased.

Another of our newspaper ads from the Jewish Telegraph.
14th August 1970.

CHAPTER 28

The Works Outing

It was the time when bonding was the catchword. The government had encouraged the bosses to be more approachable to their staff to let them know that we were human and so on. We were encouraged maybe to have a little social intercourse. There had been plenty of the other going on in our place over the years and, besides, we were all the same species after all. Human that is. I had felt deprived. Everyone was going on works dinners, theatre, ballet, opera and all sorts of cultural activities. Why shouldn't J A Hyman join in?

All my staff, well most, had worked hard over the previous twelve months and deserved some recognition. I decided that maybe an outing for everyone, a works outing, would be good for bonding and to get to know each other outside of the confines of a work environment but to have a free and unrestricted educational evening. An evening when, perhaps, we could discuss the problems of the world and maybe put them right.

I asked the fish frying girls what they thought of the idea. They were a little apprehensive. After all they, that is the four of them, had never been outside Salford except for coming to work in Waterloo Road, amazing but true. Their idea of a good night out was a trip to the local pub with their loved ones, partners or even husbands, drink four or five pints followed by chasers. The men would knock back about ten or even twelve pints of Stella, affectionately, but not sure if this is the right definition, referred to as the Wife Beater. There would then inevitably be a fall out followed by a good punch up, a few cuts, black eyes and bruised lips. Then on to the restaurant for a doner kebab with chips, salt and vinegar of course, a couple of vodkas to wash the kebab down and then a good seeing to, as the locals called a leg over across the kitchen table and then stagger to bed for a well-earned rest. I will relate their story at some later date, but I digress.

The butchers and the shop staff were up for it too. So it was agreed we would go on a works outing. The problem was where to go and how to get there and, of course, back. I didn't want to lose anyone or for them to become so rat-arsed that they would not be able to work the next day. With this in mind I chose a Thursday, as Fridays were not particularly busy as the working week was virtually over and Friday being payday they would have to turn up for their wages. We traditionally always finished early so they could go to the pub, bookies, shopping, tallyman and me to go to synagogue!

We owned three shops on the block, numbers one two and four, number three being owned by a guy called Ron. This shop was the local chip shop. It had started life as The Waterloo Chippy but over the years the locals had nicked some of the letters on the sign, presumably for education purposes and had left it as The loo ippy. Ron had never changed the sign as he reckoned that if his customers thought that it was a Chinese chip shop and if they were happy with that so be it.

Ron's best seller and local delicacy was chips and curry sauce. The fact being that the polystyrene tray tasted better than the contents on it was indeed acclamation to Ron's culinary skills. It is a local folklore that Egon Ronay passed by once but it was never confirmed. In fact when Ron decided to retire some years later we bought his shop and when it was boarded up during the refurbishment some local wag daubed on the boards: 'Jews Out bring back Ron the Chinky'. It showed how far down the local pecking order we had come. Ron, by the way, had as much Chinese blood in him as I had.

The reason I mentioned Ron was that he had transport in the shape of a twenty-seater bus, which was used to transport his potatoes and other necessary things to run a chippy and he was happy to be our official driver on the outing.

Being a democratic organisation, I decided that we should go to the Blackpool Illuminations. This was greeted with unanimous approval and excitement. I would pay the petrol for the trip and meal. I had booked a gourmet fish and chip shop supper in Fleetwood, which would be our first port of call. After soaking up the atmosphere of Fleetwood we would then travel in a southerly direction, through the illuminations to the pleasure beach, where there would be a one hour break to wet ones whistle or whatever turned you on, or for the partaking of any kind of ride that took your fancy. There would be one stop on the M61 services for an essential break and then back home to their loved ones and husbands or wives.

There was now the most important issue to sort out and that was the booze. After all, a dry works outing would not be an outing at all. It was decided that there would be a money collection from everyone for booze and whatever they collected I would double. They managed some £80. From where on a Thursday no one knew! And I didn't ask. When doubled by me we then had the princely sum of £160, which in the 1980s was equivalent to a very lot of liquor. I reckoned that it was going to be an eventful night.

The day finally arrived and after a hard day's work it was time to board our trusty yellow van with windows and, of course, seats. There were plenty of questions, like did we need passports? What time would we be arriving back home? What would happen if we lost someone? And so on. The answers being no, I don't know and I don't know. That seemed to satisfy everyone and so off we went, the first stop being the local off-licence.

Luckily our vehicle had a large carrying capacity as the rear seats were completely filled with crates of Joseph Holt Salford, a local beer, and Boddingtons Manchester ale. The journey started very quietly and rapidly gained momentum as bottles and cans were consumed. At first chatter and then it became louder and finally the chat turned, as if by magic into song, firstly melodious then more raucous until the first sighting of the famous Blackpool tower and then the bus really started rocking. Arriving at our restaurant in Fleetwood I informed everyone that we had one hour and they should try and pace themselves as the night was only just beginning and we didn't want to lose anyone to the demon drink or anything else.

A nourishing and healthy calorie controlled banquet ensued consisting of thick battered cod and chips served with Manchester caviar which, for the uninformed, is mushy peas.

Peter Thick brown sauce and lashings of bread and butter followed by a large piece of apple pie with cream all washed down with a pint mug of steaming hot tea. Ah bliss!

A head count ensued and as we had a missing person a search party was sent out to look for little Sue, who was eventually found in the loo. The night out was beginning to become a little stressful, maybe this wasn't such a good idea after all. Finally, with everyone back on the bus, we headed South through Thornton Cleveleys, past the majestic Norbreck Hydro hotel which, as everyone knows, was built to resemble something like a sort of castle. The girls said that it was architecturally wonderful and reminded them of Windsor castle they had seen on the tele and did the Queen stay there when she visited Blackpool. I replied that I would ask her when we next met.

The bus slowly trundled on with lots of oohs and ahhs at every magnificent tableau of lights. Eventually, reaching the Pleasure Beach, the high point of the evening is where the months of planning would come in. There would be an hour and a half to sample the delights of the funny house, big dipper, mighty waltzer and all the other nauseating rides which, as a child I thought were great but, as an older and maybe a little wiser person had begun to think otherwise. However, it was a works outing not a Stan night out.

Strict instructions were issued to meet at the fun house after the ninety minute slot and not be late or we would not be back home in Manchester until very late and after all there was work tomorrow. This was not received very well but assurances were given that everyone would turn up on time.

Alas, assurances counted for very little with that lethal combination of crazy rides, candy floss, kiss me quick hats, and demon booze in the bewitching atmosphere of the pleasure beach. Sure enough at the allotted departure time there was only Ron and me. It took another hour to round everyone up, by which time I had made an executive decision that this would be the last works outing during my tenure as the keeper of J.A. Hyman. As the final one was rounded up it reminded me of that popular television programme of the time Bonanza, except I wasn't rounding them up taking them to market but merely trying to get them home safe and sound.

How everyone had managed to drink so much was a complete mystery to me. After one and a half pints of beer I needed the loo every few minutes but I suppose it was down to years of dedicated training, or maybe a diet of batter, chips and curry sauce sufficiently soaked up the beer enabling them to hold their liquor. Only medical science could give the answer. And medical science data was definitely not available on that night.

We finally went on our way, the singing becoming more raucous as yet more alcohol was consumed until we arrived at our penultimate stop at the Chorley service station on the M61. By this time bladders must have been at bursting point because as soon as our trusty vehicle stopped there was a mad dash for the exit with the sole aim of getting to the toilets before it was too late. As usual it had been raining and there were large puddles in the car park and yes it happened to one of the girls who was to say the least a little tipsy. As she reached the door of the bus the cold air and rain hit her and she just sort of fell out of the entrance and did a belly flop right into a large muddy puddle of water, much to the amusement of everyone else on board. Thank goodness I didn't have to dry her down and luckily only her pride was hurt but it did sober everyone up and thankfully everyone returned back to our trusty bus in quick time suitably toileted. We thankfully arrived back home and delivered everyone back to their loved ones safe and sound. I took a huge breath and went home repeating to myself 'Never again, never again…..'

CHAPTER 29

Pesach - Again

It had been a busy Christmas, or should it be Xmas or winter holiday. Our Jewish authorities did not recognise the first two but they sure appreciated the extra revenue it brought them in. It was all over and we were in a new and exciting year. What would it bring and what had we to look forward to? Quiet days, freezing hands, big bills and, looming in the distance, bad tempers, stress, lots of shouting, tearing at hair, lack of sleep, worry. Yes, the dreaded Pesach. It was, to state the obvious, a taxing time.

Every year I pondered whether it was worth all the fuss and bother to plan and prepare. What convinced me that it was a necessity was the need not to let the local communities of Manchester and the North West down as they relied on us for all their Passover requirements. After all, they had supported us throughout the previous year therefore it was our obligation to prepare and put on this extravaganza for them.

Planning ahead was essential as the factory had to be cleaned and scrubbed and made kosher for the Passover reasonably early as we supplied a great proportion of the communities with our Hy-Fry fish and it had to be produced packed, distributed, ready for the stores to display and sell all in good time for the festival. The scramble to buy suitable essential ingredients was made considerably more difficult by our religious authority, as they had the final say as to what was acceptable for this year; what was fine last year was not necessarily good for this one. When they finally gave the permission for some ingredients it was found virtually every time that some other key ingredient had not yet been produced. How one was able to manufacture anything under these circumstances was, to state the obvious, difficult. I eventually became wise to this incompetence and as the only ingredients necessary to have the Passover labels for the fish production were matzo meal and pepper, I always kept a store of pepper from the previous year. Simple, but essential. It's amazing what you can achieve with a little resourcefulness. Rakusens were thankfully always on time with their matzo meal. First problem solved.

Being under supervision of our local Beth Din, meant that we always had some person who would ensure that the products we were making conformed to their exacting high standards. In the early days the standard of supervisor was of the highest calibre. I recollect a couple of the gentlemen that stand out from that time, both having survived the holocaust. Firstly there was Meyer Cahan, coming to this country, learning the language and studying accountancy whilst quietly and competently performing his supervision duties. Mr. Cahan later qualified and became our accountant for a number of years. Secondly there was Shmuel Parness, a completely different character, being French and a survivor of the camps. He introduced us to his relatives in Rue de Rosiers in Paris, who sold perfume and every time we go to Paris we still visit the same store run by the family, as a sort of pilgrimage dedicated to him. He was a highly intelligent man and a great philosopher and very quirky. I still remember one of his quotes. He always used the analogy of the rich man who took him into his grand house to show off his beautiful silver and art collection. He told Shmuel that this was his investment and should there ever be a rainy day he could then sell them. Shmuel replied that if he had to sell these investments then he was indeed a poor man, a poorer man than he was. A philosophy I have never forgotten. Alas the ravages of his life all too soon caught up with him and he passed away at a very early age and is sadly missed.

In recent times the ethos of our religious body has changed. They wanted an even better standard of kashrus (being Kosher), not a bad thing to aim for, but their investment in staff did not match up to the high standards that they aspired to. I was told that they never had enough money to employ the calibre of people who had been employed in past times and had to cut their cloth accordingly. It has always been an enigma as to how they spent the vast amounts of money that were received through fees. But that's another story.

The saying goes if you pay in peanuts you get whatever and boy did we get whatever. These guys were on the most part incompetent but certainly not impotent. They knew their Talmud and they sure knew how to study, marry and make babies but it was very much jobs for the boys and it was not the Almighty that provided for them but us. This was our metaphorical cross and we had to bear it.

So when it came to cleaning scrubbing and koshering the factory for the Passover, the girls were there to clean and the guys, The Beth Din, were there to supervise and, when awake, to help. The reason I said awake was that they had so many children that there was always one or two who would be unwell and keep them up all night, so it was easier to hide and sleep during the day. The fish frying girls had been with me for years and knew exactly what to do for the Passover clean-up. They were able to boil, scrub, dip all the equipment, which was already sparkly clean and spent the best part of a week bringing everything up to the acceptable Passover standard. The supervisors' role in the cleaning seemed to be to damage and destroy as much equipment as possible. They may have learnt all the theory but they hadn't a clue what to do in practice. Boiling water all over the place and sometimes over themselves, but even worse was the blow lamp.

This instrument was supposed to be used to burn off any residue of chometz by probing the inaccessible parts of equipment leaving the metal baskets, trays, knives, and mincer parts cleansed, ready for supervision of the Dayanim, the real big chief Rabbis who would come down to Waterloo Road for the final inspection. The problem was that these guys were not very good with blowlamps and thought it great to incinerate any piece of equipment they could lay their hands on. It was such fun! Every year without fail they destroyed some machine or other, sometimes costing the BD hundreds of pounds because I would stop payments to them until the replacement cost of the damage that the pyromaniacs had inflicted had been rectified.

Finally the day of the final inspection arrived, everyone nervously awaiting the arrival of the cavalcade of Volvo estates, the lookouts scanning up and down Waterloo Road for the first signs of the convoy. It was like the annual royal visit, without the bunting. I often wondered if they knew where the shop was situated as they never patronised it, but they managed to take our money for the supervision fees. Funny religion, it was kosher enough for us lot but not for them.

The Rabbis swept into the premises always with the same comments that the shop was a credit to us and how wonderful that there was this kosher facility for the Jewish population of Manchester. I often wondered why they never supported us and then one day I realised it was because metaphorically, I suppose, I supported Manchester City and they had their own football teams. Religiously speaking we were second division and they were premier league.

My fish girls had cleaned the factory for many years to the acceptable standards but I knew that there would always be a few RECOMMENDATIONS solely to justify the annual state visit. Then they were gone. With a 'See you next year, PG', leaving the precious red Passover labels in the hands of our immensely happy and proud supervisor. After all, he had been entrusted with these extremely important labels. It was a macho thing, something akin to having the powers of a traffic warden. He would with great pomp and ceremony carefully put them in his pocket take them home with him for safe keeping and then usually forget to bring them with him the next day.

My fish frying girls were the veritable salt of the earth. The journey to work being the farthest that they had travelled in their lives. The job and location being their oasis of calm and normality in the chaos of their own lives. If this was calm then they must have had a very sad existence at home. They were experts at the job and between them could churn out hundreds of chopped and fried fish balls all weighing the same in amazingly quick time. The result was that they always finished the job early and then sat down, brewed up and discussed all the problems of the world, as you do coming from Lower Broughton. They would sit and chat for a couple of hours or so each day and then grudgingly go back to the drudgery and demands of home life. In fact, work for them, I suppose, was paradoxically like going to a social or health club. It was relaxation and everyone was happy with this arrangement.

I remember the day well. It was the Thursday before the Passover. The fish orders were still piling in but thankfully the finishing line was in sight. Another week of mayhem and then the trauma of the family Seders. No time to think about the trials and tribulations of the impending family get together. Who would be speaking and who would not be speaking and who would depart early in a huff and who would stay? It was the same every year, it being a family thing as traditional as the four questions. But no time to ponder now as there was a still mountain of work yet to finish.

My fish girls had gone upstairs for a break, a well-earned rest, a brew and, of course, a smoke. I was running around trying to sort out shouting customers, confused staff, answering the telephone all at the same time. It was crazy but if it was not chaos it was not working.

As you would understand, being in a Jewish shop one week before Passover there would be a multitude and mêlée of Jewish shoppers and anyone not of the faith would stand out like the proverbial sore thumb. And so it was thumb-like that two official looking people, one male and the other I think female, standing within the scrum completely nonplussed enquiring as to my whereabouts. Everyone pointed in my direction and reluctantly I approached them knowing that usually officials do not do visits at busy times unless it was real trouble.

The man showed me his identification, introduced himself and colleague and said, 'DHSS fraud inspectors'. Not having a clue as to what they wanted I invited them upstairs to my office and asked them what this unannounced visit was about.

'Well Mr Hyman' said the man, I assumed he was the senior, he then asked if we had in our employ two ladies named Maureen and Doreen. I forget the surnames. In fact I never knew them as they were known to everyone

168

as Mo and Doe. He then asked me how many hours a week they worked. This was an interesting question as they were so proficient at the job they usually worked for a couple of hours a day, holidays excepted and after work they always stayed on. It was their own time, their social time, as I have explained earlier.

He then asked me if the P11D had been signed. Now I believe that this document states that this was their only job and they were not working anywhere else and were not claiming certain benefits. I seemed to recall that Jonathan, my long suffering accountant, had issued these forms to me some years before and had asked the casual employees, as they were so called then, to sign them thus covering me from committing fraud and all sorts of heinous misdemeanours. I used to, and still do, loathe any kind of office work and my dear long suffering accountant always looked after me by sorting out all the invoices, tax affairs and bookkeeping for me.

As I was telephoning Jonathan, because I did not have a clue where these pieces of paper may have been placed or where they may have even been filed, I suddenly heard the sound of pounding feet rushing down the stairs. I did not pay much attention to this, as there were all sorts of weird things happening at this crazy time. Eventually I unearthed these yellowing bits of paper and triumphantly and thankfully gave them to the DHSS man and his colleague.

They perused the documents and then asked me if these had indeed been signed by Maureen and Dorothy. I told them that as far as I was aware they had signed them but I had not paid much attention at the time. He then asked if I knew the surnames.

'I see from these forms' he said 'that they have signed as M Mouse and D Duck.'

I told them I did not have a clue, as they were only known to everyone as Mo and Doe. I was dying to burst out laughing and would have done so if the situation had not been so serious. I suddenly realised what the clattering noise down the stairs was. It was my fish fryers doing a runner and I never saw those two smashing girls again. What a tragedy. In another life what they could have been, well, who knows.

The sequel to Ms M Mouse and Ms D Duck was that the former had evidently been claiming sick benefits for the past twelve years and was taken to court where she was fined about twelve thousand pounds. She was asked to pay five pounds per week off the fine. Working out how long it would have taken, I calculated that she would be paying for some forty five years. In fact I later found out that the fine was only paid for about two months and then Mo stopped paying. I do not think that the authorities ever pursued her. Doe on the other hand had no case to answer but was too frightened to return to work. They were smashing girls, the salt of the earth and we missed them.

How we managed to complete that Passover was indeed a miracle but we did. The Almighty works in strange ways, but not on Saturdays.

Ad from the Jewish Telegraph 27ᵗʰ March 1997.

172

CHAPTER 30

DAF Lost and Found

My Mum, Jean, always did her shopping on a Tuesday. She would drive up Waterloo Road and always park on the same spot. She would leave the car right at the corner of Waterloo Road and Barrow Hill Road facing upwards towards Cheetham Hill. She had to park like this as she was not very good at driving backwards. It was the same ritual, always the same day and always at the same time.

The car that she drove was a car made in Holland. It was a little red two-door affair that was simplicity itself to drive. To drive it you pushed the gear stick forward to go forward and pulled the stick backwards to go backwards and somewhere in the middle of pushing and pulling was neutral, the concept of which she never quite grasped. The car had as one of its many extras a handbrake and an ashtray.

The ashtray was well used as my Mum always had a fag in her mouth especially whilst driving. She did finally kick this habit, as I mentioned before, when she reached the age of ninety-one as she thought it might damage her health in later life. But at this time in her mid-eighties she still enjoyed her cigarettes and why not?

The handbrake was an unused item in the car; a bit of a nuisance really as she always managed to entangle her coat around this unnecessary piece of superfluous equipment and then have to be untangled.

The most useful accessory was this thing that when pulled out from the dashboard was perfect for hanging her handbag on. Her best friend Freda Brown had told her this. The only trouble with that was it made the car go funny so she said and seemed to create lots of blue smoke from the exhaust. This we discovered was in fact the choke, definitely not for handbags but, as all the oldies will know, was for helping the car to start when the engine was cold. This amazing little red car was a DAF which, by the way, survived until it was passed down to the second grandchild who eventually managed to destroy it.

Mum was always made welcome whilst visiting her former emporium and she enjoyed chatting to all the staff. Many had been there for years and were accustomed to her weekly visits. She used to tell them of the time when Dad and her had started the business just after the Second World War. It had been a truly acrimonious time for them both as Dad had been fighting for king and country and when he finally returned from three years in India he had not been made very welcome by his siblings and their spouses, who had lived off the fat of the land and certainly did not want to share anything with the youngest boy child. Eventually after many difficulties, trials and tribulations the business was split up and Mum and Dad finished up with the store in Waterloo Road, which at that time was still a Jewish area.

A few years later they opened their second shop in Lapwing Lane, Didsbury, which Mum looked after. She was a hard worker, a true grafter, she took no prisoners and ran the shop with a feisty enthusiasm. She unfortunately did not move with the times and ran the store as if there was still rationing, which was fine when there was but not so good when there was not. Everyone in South Manchester knew Hymans and, of course, Jean and they still talk about the Hyman era in Didsbury for the great shop that she provided for the community at that time.

It was a couple of weeks before the Jewish New Year and it is an annual tradition that relatives visit the cemeteries to pay respects to their loved ones who were no longer here. I had received a phone call earlier in the day asking me if it was alright for us to accommodate a visit from the Blackpool and St. Anne's Friendship Club, as they had had a vote and the members of the club had democratically decided to do a three centre visit to Manchester that particular year.

The coach would start at Heathlands Elderly Care Home where they would have lunch. Then visit the various local cemeteries to pay their respects and a little prayer for their departed families and friends and finally the highlight of the day, J A Hyman Titanics, where they would be able to use the toilets, a major plus as I have found out in later life. Have a good *shmie* round, which is a good browse, have a sandwich and drink and buy any goods that they fancied to take home with them. I told my staff to forget going home at the usual time and be prepared for anything and everything out of the ordinary. It was going to be an eventful day and evening.

Meanwhile Mum had finished her weekly shop and was saying her goodbyes to everyone. I carried her bags out of the shop to where she had parked her car. It was not there. Going back into the store I asked her if she had broken with tradition and parked somewhere else. She replied that indeed she had not, she had always left the car in the same place and today was no exception. I rapidly came to the conclusion that her little red Daf had been nicked. Why anyone should want to steal that particular car was a mystery as it was not a robber's getaway car, unless it was Noddy and Big Ears, the top speed being about forty mile an hour and that was on a good day with the wind behind.

A plaintive phone call to the police explaining where the car had been parked and that some hardened local criminal had stolen my Mum's car, presumably to commit a dastardly deed, maybe even a bank job, or joy riders just to burn rubber. The police pretended not to be too interested but I am sure that they were. I was told that they would deal with the situation with due urgency and would be in touch with us as soon as they had some meaningful information. My Mum dejectedly sat in the office with a cup of tea, wondering who could have perpetrated such a dastardly deed to some little old lady's car.

Thirty minutes passed and suddenly a phone call. Mum shouted thank the Lord it must be the police who have found my poor little car. But it wasn't, it was Mrs. Cohen wanting to give a fish order for the holidays. Abject misery from Mum and then another call this time it was from the police. They had found the car. Mum was so excited. They have rescued my little Daf from a life of crime. I hope that it is not damaged in any way. I asked her not to become too excited as the policeman told me where the car had been located. He then said that he and his colleague would call immediately at the shop to talk to my mother regarding this incident.

Sure enough a couple of minutes later a police squad car stopped outside and two six foot coppers emerged and enquired as to the whereabouts of this Mrs. Hyman. They were shown into the office. Mum was overjoyed to be receiving news of her beloved car and was quite indignant that someone had had the temerity to take it.

'Thank you for finding it so quickly' she told them. 'Has it been used for a job?'

The policeman explained that the car had not been used for a job as she had called it but was involved in a crime. Mum said,

'If there had been a crime committed then there had to be a criminal.'

'Exactly!' said the policeman 'and I am afraid that I have to give you a caution and anything you say may be taken down in evidence and used in court…'

Mother went all indignant at this point and asked what on earth for. The policeman explained that the beloved car, which had been facing up the hill in the direction of Cheetham, had evidently not had its handbrake on. That's the lever in the middle that kept tangling up her overcoat. The car had very gently rolled down the Waterloo Road hill, not hitting anything on its way down, which was a miracle in itself and had come to a standstill in the middle of the extremely busy Bury New Road, causing traffic jams of two miles in each direction. The ensuing chaos even warranted a mention on national traffic updates on the radio and drivers had been advised to keep away from the area.

I went to the bottom of the road with one of the police officers to reunite car with driver whilst the other police officer issued the ticket for driving without due care and attention to a shaken but much relieved mother. Not quite as bad as Aunty Ena, who had run over some poor policeman's foot whilst on point duty a few years previously but a good story nevertheless and thankfully with a happy ending. (Point duty was used when traffic lights broke down; a policeman would stand in the middle of a road junction directing the traffic.)

It was time to turn our attention to the afternoon visit, having reunited Mum with her car and sent her safely on her way. The friendship club were due at three-ish according to their itinerary, so we knew it could be around four when they would arrive. Sure enough, at four fifteen this fifty-seater coach arrived on the forecourt and out tottered thirty seven happy and excited Fylde coast senior citizens expecting to sample the delights of the North's finest delicatessen store.

The driver informed me of the correct number that had entered and said that it was necessary as he would have to do a count on the way back to make sure that no one was missing. How right he was.

Cups of tea, smoked salmon sandwiches and cakes were handed out to our travelling guests and then down to business. They, bless them, were game to buy virtually anything and everything. What we don't appreciate living in Manchester is the range and choice of kosher foods in all the stores and the selection of places where we can shop for them. All this is taken for granted. Travel a couple of miles out of the area and it is a virtual desert for any aspect of Jewish life. So this was their day and they were going to take full advantage of it, even if their families had all grown up, moved on to other towns and now had families of their own. They were going to stock up even if most of the goods that they bought were of no use to them. On reflection I suppose it was the same as us going to Blackpool and buying sticks of rock which were never going to be eaten but at the time it was good fun choosing all the different colours.

One incident sticks out as I recall, Mrs Cohen wanted to choose her own *shmaltz* herring and was having a heated conversation with one of the girls, who had told her that she was not allowed to stick her hand in the herring barrel to choose her own fish. Mrs Cohen had rejected every herring that the poor girl had fished out for her and before anyone had the time to say you're not allowed do that, Mrs Cohen rolled up the sleeves on her mink coat and stuck her arm inside the barrel and after a few seconds emerged with a herring. She told the bewildered girl, 'This is the one I want!' The assistant asked what on earth the difference was as all herrings were the same as far as she was concerned. The lady explained to her that she only wanted a male herring as the milt was lovely and soft to eat as the female herring had a hard roe which was totally inedible. The lady then delicately wiped her arm down with a tissue, rolled down the sleeve of her mink coat and carried on with her shopping.

After the shopping frenzy, which ensured a jolly good day's takings, it was time for the group to return to their coach. The round up was on.

Some thirty minutes later, thirty-five friendship clubbers were collected from the various nooks and crannies of 123 Waterloo Road and were safely back on the bus. Two had disappeared and nobody knew where they were. A search party eventually found the missing persons. Thankfully no one had fallen into the smoke oven or the pickle barrels. Yes, you may have guessed correctly. They were locked in the toilets, one in the ladies and one in the gents, not both together thankfully and were finally rescued without the assistance of the fire brigade.

Fully watered and not too distressed, they were escorted to the bus and sent on their way back to Blackpool. A good time had been had by all.

CHAPTER 31

Just Another Crazy Day

I know that the Pesach stories keep cropping up, but over a time scale of some forty odd years there had to be lots of crazy incidents and I remember a couple of them that had, coincidentally, happened on the same day.

It was the usual chaos just before Passover, customers milling, staff shouting, drivers trying to deliver goods, the ladies, bless them, trying to park their cars as near to the front door as was humanly possible - not for the problem of schlepping, or even the loading of their cars, but just in case God forbid it started to rain whilst shopping and the consequences of getting their hair wet and ruining that new hair-do was, as every one of us males understands, disastrous, to state the obvious.

Let me paint a picture. The scene was akin to an industrious beehive. Workers and, of course, lots of Jewish Queens. So, with the Pesach frenzy and tempers running high something had to happen and it did. At this time a Mrs P., whom I will relate to as Barbara, a very attractive and feisty lady weaved her way on to the forecourt in her brand new Renault, parked neatly and found a trolley. By the way, we operated at that time a trolley rescue service; we gave home to abandoned supermarket trolleys and at that particular time had several Kwiksave and Netto trolleys, not to mention the upmarket ones that had been rescued from a life of crime or from a watery grave in the River Irk. I can't understand why I was never recognised by the Queen or anyone else for my services in helping save the local environment and giving these poor abandoned trolleys a good home. Barbara had found a Kwiksave 95 four wheels, all working in sync, a rarity, and had started on the exciting journey of her Passover shop.

At this time a huge wagon had drawn up on the road, as there was no room on the forecourt for him to park. This was the eagerly awaited wine and spirit order especially for Passover from Palwin wines.

Our man Wayne, with the help of the forklift truck proceeded to unload the pallets of this Passover nectar. However, on taking off the last pallet he must have let his attention wander or was thinking about his important darts match later that evening and instead of lowering the fifty five cases times twelve bottles of no. 4A wine to within six inches of the ground as was the correct procedure, he decided on the scenic route. That was carrying this very heavy load nine feet off the ground. One tiny hump on the forecourt and guess what? The fifty-five cases tipped over with a shattering crash. All six hundred and sixty bottles landing on or in the very close proximity of Mrs. Barbara P's brand new Renault, causing a reasonable amount of damage and changing the shape of the car quite considerably for ever.

Meanwhile our Barbara was completing her Passover shop quite oblivious to the carnage and mayhem that had only just happened in the outside world. The question was, who would pluck up the courage to inform Barbara of the damage on, in and around her new car. In the meantime I had rung up the insurance broker and by some strange coincidence my broker of many years standing just happened to be the good lady's son in law.

If I recall, the conversation started like this:

'Good afternoon, Bridge Insurance, Paula here, how can I help?' I told her that there had been an accident and she asked me for the details in order to issue a claims form. What was the make of car and I told her that it was a Renault, the reg, colour and so on and the name of the owner and I told her that it was a Mrs P. She asked me the driver's first name and I told her that it was Barbara and suddenly she went very quiet.

'Hello?' I shouted down the phone 'Are you still there?' and all I received was,

'You said that the driver was a Mrs Barbara P? Oh shit!'

'Yes that's right. It's Mike's mother-in-law'.

I waited until Barbara had completed her shopping, sat her down and informed her what had happened. She asked to see Wayne the forklift driver to ask him what he had done to her brand new car but to add to my woes Wayne had done what all good cowards do. He had done a runner and was nowhere to be seen.

I tried a little humour to try and ease the tension whilst awaiting rescue from her husband, telling the poor unfortunate lady that only twelve or so bottles of the wine had actually gone through the windscreen and it was the best quality wine being number 4A. I said that she should liken it to the launching of a large ship being blessed with champagne. The other few hundred bottles had landed on various parts of the car making an interesting colour combination.

She was not amused at my attempted humour, but very graciously accepted my profound apologies and after a cup of tea ventured outside to look at the carnage, which by now had attracted a large crowd of locals and customers wondering what on earth had created this mayhem, with the river of wine slowly wending and the aroma wafting down Waterloo Road. She immediately returned inside categorically stating (the vocabulary has been changed as there may be young folk reading this) that she would never drive that car again. She was true to her word and she never did drive that poor unfortunate car ever again. I had had enough excitement for one afternoon but it was turning out to be a double whammy day.

There was not enough time to dwell on the misfortunes of the unfortunate Mrs. P's car as there were still so many problems to sort out. The Passover chocolates had not arrived from the local wholesaler, Messrs Goldstein. Why they should be delivered so late has always been a mystery to me as there was always a two-year sell-by date on them. Maybe the Goldsteins did not want anyone to eat them too early and then have no *nash* left for the Passover. I did secretly feel sorry for them, as every shop wanted all the Passover goods first to steal a march on the opposition. Hysterical shopkeepers driving them almost demented to be the first delivery.

About five thirty that afternoon Goldstein's truck finally arrived with a very stressed Goldstein driving. Now David Goldstein was normally a very calm and placid person, but the stress of the Passover frenzy had finally taken its toll on him and he had the look of some poor demented being who was about to or who had lost it. Whatever it was, it had gone. The poor guy was in such a bad way he very nearly accepted a cup of tea from one of our girls who saw the state he was in, then suddenly realised that maybe the milk was not kosher enough for him and he politely declined. All he wanted to do was to unload our chocolates and move on as quickly as possible for his next delivery.

Trying to unload and check off these chocolates with throngs of customers diving into the packing cases was virtually impossible. Working on the theory that the Goldsteins were an honest and upstanding family, and assuming they had delivered what we had ordered and were subsequently signed for as correct, the much harassed Mr. David G. ran out of the shop, jumped into his wagon and accelerated away from the shop as fast as his truck would go. The only problem being that David in his haste to be on his way had forgotten to close the tailgate and shutters of his truck.

As he headed up the road box upon box and bar upon bar of Kosher For Passover chocolates were thrown from the open back end of the truck and were strewn on to the road. From nowhere hundreds of children appeared stopping all the traffic and stuffing and carrying bars and boxes of chocolates wherever they could be stuffed and carried. It may have been Passover for us but it was a very early Christmas for these kids. This carnage continued until the entire consignment had been deposited on the road. It was like the scene from a film. Kids and then adults leaving their cars and passengers on a bus all joining in this chocolate frenzy. The ensuing traffic chaos attracted the attention of our local policeman who stood helplessly by the roadside watching this amazing scene unfold.

In the meantime the hapless Mr. Goldstein continued on his way, unaware of the chaos he was causing and the happiness he was making for the locals. When he stopped at his next delivery destination and looked in astonishment at the rear of his empty truck and immediately realising what had happened he quickly turned round and retraced his steps back down to Waterloo Road but alas all he found was a load of empty chocolate box cartons strewn across the road and, to add insult to injury, the local bobby who gave him a ticket for creating litter, a huge traffic jam and having an insecure load.

Poor David, it was definitely not his day. But it had been a great street party for the kids. The chocolates must have tasted good, even the strawberry cream ones that nobody likes. And I was never offered any cheap Jewish chocolates from any of the local scallies.

So I can safely assume that they were all eaten up. I'm sure our Rabbis would have approved and been proud that the entire population of Waterloo Road had eaten kosher on that particular day.

Our Titanics paper bag.

CHAPTER 32

Is It Kosher?

How would I have anything to write about without the amazing idiosyncrasies of our wonderful Beth Din? If they were football referees no one would ever score a goal because they would always move the goalposts. Just as you were going to score the rules would be changed and the ball would harmlessly go out for a goal kick.

I will try and illustrate with issues that happened to us. In our strange religion an oven or any implement used for the cooking of food must be lit by a person of the Jewish faith. The reasoning for this strange rule is that if some unscrupulous person not of the faith lit or switched on the appliance unsupervised then maybe they could slip some non-kosher product into the food being cooked, therefore making it *treife*. Why anyone would want to do anything like this or even reason it out is way beyond my comprehension. However a rule is a rule and has to be observed.

Jeff Holland, the manager of our Cheadle shop, had been working in the kosher butchery trade all his working life. He began his career and learnt his trade from the age of fifteen at Kregers butchers shop in Lapwing Lane, Didsbury. After working there for ten years and becoming a master butcher he went to our Cheadle shop and managed it for some thirty-five years before retiring for a well-earned peaceful existence. He had therefore a wealth of experience in dealing with all kashrut matters and his knowledge of the kosher rules and regulations regarding meat was as good as anyone.

The supervisors working for the Beth Din were notoriously bad time keepers. The job was definitely not a vocation for them as most treated it as a vacation and considered their position as a divine right to do what they wanted as and when they pleased. One morning after waiting for over an hour for the supervisor to turn up for work and a very important order awaiting for four cooked chickens to be roasted on the spit, the driver pacing and waiting impatiently to deliver the cooked chickens to the St. Anne's community along with their weekly orders, Jeff made an executive decision. He called Yossi Cohen, who ran the adjacent shop, and asked him if he would put the plug in the socket and switch on the rotisserie.

Some forty-five minutes later the supervisor sauntered in to work. The usual excuses, learning until late and with lots of children, some not sleeping and keeping him awake. Mumbled apology and sleepily went off to make himself a cup of tea. Suddenly the supervisor realised that the chicken rotisserie was in full flow and the chickens were practically cooked. Without asking who had switched the chicken spit on, he rushed off to the public telephone box down the road to report this heinous crime of a non-believer to a higher authority.

Sure enough some sixty minutes later the full deputation of the hierarchy from the Beth Din arrived, resplendent in long black coats and large intimidating hats, all sporting the mandatory flowing beards.

The first thing that they did on their arrival was to summon me immediately to the store in South Manchester. No explanations being given or reasons for this visit, everything in the shop having been put on hold. On my arrival I was greeted by the large body of rabbis along with a very perplexed Mr Holland.

They would not tell him the reason for this visit but waited until I had arrived. They said that there had been a serious breach of the kosher laws because a non-Jewish person had started the cooking process and they were going to make all the cooked chickens in the store *treife* and furthermore, under no circumstances would they tolerate such a blatant breach of the rules again.

They then asked Mr Jeff if he understood and if he had anything to say. He explained to them that their supervisor had been so late for work that he had asked Mr

Cohen from next door to plug in the chicken rotisserie and to press the relevant buttons as the supervisor had not turned up for work and they had a very urgent order to send to St Anne's and did not want to make all the deliveries late. This startling news that indeed a person of the faith had done the switching took the proverbial wind from their sails and after going in a huddle told us that this had changed the situation and we could now sell these cooked chickens and could carry on as normal. This was very kind of them, as they had disrupted a complete day for everyone besides a scare for me, as I did not know the cause of the original problem.

A letter was received a couple of days later underlining the problem of lighting and starting the cookers and I suggested a very simple remedy to their predicament. A time switch that would automatically switch on all forms of cookers at the same time every morning. After three months of deliberation this proposal was accepted and thankfully the next cooking crisis was averted without the need of a Cohen. Maybe with a little bit of common sense! But there would always be something else and there was.

Some time after the cooked chicken incident there was another poultry problem, this time on a much smaller scale. The birds in question being quail. It is thought that these birds were the ancestors of the very same variety that descended down as manna for the children of Israel long ago, as they trudged across the desert for a lot of years way back in biblical times.

A telephone call and another great bargain for the Manchester community. Was I interested in a few thousand quail? All with the Paris Beth Din supervision kosher certification label. The price seemed to be good. A bit of haggling, and we were then the proud owners of three thousand frozen quail packed in pairs. Presumably, male and female just like in biblical times when it had rained a lot and they had embarked on an epic boat ride.

It's amazing how many little quail fit into a freezer and at two for £5.00 it was a wonderful opportunity for the good people of Manchester to be creative and introduce some-sophistication to the gourmet Shabbat dinner; have a change from the humdrum of a Friday night chicken supper. It was amazing how many wonderful recipes the women of Manchester thought up in that particular quail season.

Everything was good, the quail sale was bringing in new customers who were willing to try a new approach to their culinary art and impress their friends with new and innovative recipes. Business was good. What could go wrong? I went home on that particular Friday night, contented, a good week and a job well done. I have always maintained that the highlight of my week was Jennifer's chopped liver on a Friday night and then the week would rapidly decline until the following Friday when the cycle would start again because the unexpected would often happen and that following Monday it did.

At ten in the morning I looked up to the sight of the familiar Volvos being driven by our good friends from the Manchester Beth Din and heard the swooshing of their beards as they ran into the shop. I could never understand why they always rush around as if there was never enough time to complete the Lord's work on earth before they embarked to the next world to dash around all over again.

The problem they explained were the quail,

'They are not kosher and therefore you must stop selling them immediately!'

I tried to explain that they had the supervision of the Paris Beth Din on them and had been approved and accepted by the London authorities. Then the bombshell. They explained that although the other religious authorities had accepted the fact that these little birds were kosher, they did not. No satisfactory explanation was ever given. Some twenty years later I still can't understand which direction they were coming from. It was definitely not from above. The only conclusion that was reached was that if you lived south of Stoke the quail were kosher and north of the imaginary line they were not. So if it's exotic quail that you are after either move to the Sinai desert and await a miracle or move a little further south.

Yours confused, Manchester.

CHAPTER 33

Steve, Protector of the Faith

Steve came to work for me in the 1990s. He was the spitting image of Homer Simpson, being little and bald. He worked as our warehouse man and helped with all general duties that befitted this position. Steve was a generous and kind person, a great father whose children thought the world of him. He also looked after Brian, who had special needs, like the proverbial mother hen.

Brian had been shopping for years with his Mum Ethel and the dog, podgy Fred. An interesting name for the dog as Fred had no undercarriage and was therefore a lady. This fact did not faze Ethel so Fred it was. Every Tuesday they would turn up at the same time with the same routine. Ethel would leave Fred outside. She would wait for her four ounce portion of pressed beef and a pickled cucumber, sweet and sour of course, which preserved her status as being the fattest dog in the area. Brian would stand beside his Mum with head bowed and not speak or even look around him. This weekly ritual went on for years until I suggested to Ethel that maybe we could help each other. Brian could help us in the shop and this in turn would not only help Ethel, but give him a meaningful life and be a great help to us. I am pleased to say that the experiment worked and he flourished.

Our Brian had this uncanny gift of remembering every detail of every customer who had ever been through the door, remembering their hairstyle and the clothes that they had worn on previous visits and who they had been shopping with. He would help the customers out with their purchases in exchange for videos, tapes, CDs, books or in fact anything that he would spot in their cars. He became part of the fabric of the building and as I write this in 2014 Brian is still helping and collecting things. Things mean things - that is any object in a car that was not screwed down was fair game for his collection. Maybe one day he will have a sale of all his accumulated goods and receive a fortune for them. And jolly good luck to him.

Steve had taken to Brian and showed kindness and affection towards him. He always made sure that he had clean and presentable clothing and was properly fed and escorted him to work and back home. He was a willing and hard working person and was responsible and honest. That was the good Steve.

The other side of him was the one that battled with the demon drink. He could knock back up to ten cans of

Special Brew lager in one session, which was bad enough but this was, alas, during a working day. So come five o'clock the only way to find him was to follow the empty can trail. There would a very merry Steve sitting in the cellar singing gently to himself amongst the cases of olives and pickled cucumbers. He would be led up the stairs, making sure that he had his coat on, point him in the direction of home and off he would stagger. These drinking sessions could go on for weeks and we would not see him during this time. So the question is, how did he keep his job? When he was sober which was, in fairness, for months at a time he was a great jovial character. Besides being kind to Brian, he was hardworking, loyal and had a great sense of humour, which was essential in our crazy business so I always forgave his transgressions with the demon drink.

From time to time we had problems with our neighbours. The reason being was that the council, in their wisdom, moved difficult families from one estate to another, presumably to give everyone a fair share of the misery that they brought to that particular neighbourhood at that particular time. After a certain number of antisocial incidents they would move them on to some other poor sods to inflict their own particular misery and make their lives hell. Until they were again moved on and rehoused.

The children blossomed from little pests to big thugs as they grew up. Unfortunately it must have been our turn to have these families living round the corner. The petty crime rate went up even more than the Cheetham average and they made all the locals' lives miserable with the vandalism and their antisocial behaviour.

Every day there were taunts from these kids. At first, silly little things, like running in to the shop and calling the staff names and then running away. This went on for a while until they became bored as everyone ignored them and considered them as nuisances who would eventually get fed up and move on to some other kind of fun.

Then the kids changed tactics and they started making racist remarks to the customers, as they were about to park their cars to do their shopping and harassing them on their way out. They would then run away, making life unpleasant for everyone. I could never understand why they were never at school. Evidently their parents didn't care and were not interested in what they were up to during the daytime. There was no point in having the police involved as firstly they seemed powerless to become involved and secondly they weren't the slightest bit interested as these incidents must have been very low on their priority lists.

Unfortunately for us the situation was getting out of hand and was making everyday life quite uncomfortable.

One particular Sunday morning they had assembled outside the shop for a bit more anti-social behaviour and a little Jew baiting, as this seemed the only game that these social misfits were capable of. They seemed unaware as to what normal children's activities were. The parents were definitely not interested in their welfare and must have told them to play out in the street or anywhere every day so as not to be responsible for them or their actions. They were on their own and had to make their own entertainment. And they were having a great time.

This went on until Steve happened to help a customer out with her shopping and they started shouting anti-Semitic remarks aimed primarily at him. Steve, who was a Protestant, came back in to the shop and told me that he had had enough of their disgusting behaviour and he asked whether he could go home and bring back one of his drinking mates so that they could between them chase off the kids and if they could catch one or two maybe give them a good smacking, as they say in Hightown.

Half an hour later Steve returned with his mate Jock, the veteran of many a street battle. You could tell by the amount of scars on his face and the very fact of having an ear bitten off during one of his pub brawls, that he was a good ally and tough street fighter when sober. As this was the Lord's Day and it was only eleven o'clock in the morning, he was still firing on all cylinders, so to speak. He definitely was not the type of bloke that you would wish to meet on some dark and foggy night, or for that matter on some rainy Sunday morning in Hightown.

The two chased the kids off the forecourt. Luckily not being quick enough to catch any of them. The kids ran off shouting that they were going to get their Dads to sort out Steve and Jock. Just threats so we thought and order seemed to have been restored. The two of them returned to the shop and Steve produced a bottle of vodka from his pocket and they both had a celebratory drink or two.

Some fifteen minutes later there was a lot of shouting on the forecourt outside the shop. Looking out of the window I could see four big guys on the forecourt baying for the blood of Steve and Jock, the two guys who had upset their precious little ones. If they had the balls to come outside and pick on someone their own size they shouted and not terrorise harmless little children they would teach them a lesson that they would never forget. I thought it the right time to ring up the police who told me that they would come as soon as they had a car available. Waterloo Road was never high on their priority list.

Whilst on the 'phone Steve and Jock, now fortified with early Sunday morning vodka, went out to face the fathers of our tormentors. They squared up, four big guys on one side and two little ones, Jock right behind Steve on the other side. The four big ones approached Steve menacingly and at that moment Steve brought out from under his coat a rather large, mean looking machete, this being the fashionable weapon of choice at the time. The four guys on seeing this formidable weapon raised above Steve's head decided not to enter into battle with this vodka crazed little guy, and his mate so they took seconds as they say in Cheetham and did a runner.

Unfortunately Jock, who was standing directly behind Steve, was unluckily and I may add accidently hit on the head by the machete that Steve was wielding and blood was pouring down his face from a nasty gash on his baldhead.

I thought to myself as I rushed out with some towels to try and stop the blood from flowing as to why I could not have an ordinary day like any other ordinary person. Seeing the size of the cut at close range it did not need an expert to deduce that poor unfortunate Jock needed hospital treatment and several stitches for his wound. Gathering a large quantity of towels we placed the hapless Jock surrounded by all the towels with a remorseful Steve, who was holding a towel on his friends head to stem the flow of blood whilst sobering up very quickly, into the back of my car and we sped off towards A&E at Crumpsall hospital, as it was known then, as fast and carefully as my injured passenger's condition would allow. The idea was to take them to the hospital and then I would leave Steve to look after his mate and take him home in a taxi financed by me so I could go back to work.

Just having crossed Elizabeth Street and wending my way up Waterloo Road thinking that the present bizarre situation could not become any worse with two fellows in the back of my car, one of whom was covered in blood, to my horror I spied in my rear view mirror two police cars, blue lights flashing, coming up fast behind me. I thought that maybe they were on their way to a crime, but as one raced in front of me and the other stayed behind and boxed me in, just like the police chases on the television, I realised that I was the crime.

We were asked to leave the car and I was told to sit in the squad car and explain what had happened. Steve and Jock were questioned on the pavement, presumably so that the blood would not drip in the police car. And it was only when Jock fainted from loss of blood that they decided to summon an ambulance. This eventually arrived and Steve, Jock and a policeman were whisked off to Crumpsall hospital.

No charges were ever pressed on Steve or Jock. The moral of the story is do not stand directly behind a man wielding a machete otherwise it may have a bloody ending.

CHAPTER 34

Ice Cool Jazz

Jazz lived on the next block up from our shop in Waterloo Road. He was and still is a good looking guy with a very cheeky smile. He has always considered himself as a bit of a lad, always ready to do a deal and was locally renowned for his dodgy, alleged sexually explicit DVDs - all for sale at a fiver. Sadly, they rarely worked as they had been the copies of copies of pirate DVDs and were so bad that all was left to the imagination, apart from a few moans and groans on the crackly sound track, was what could have been and what should have been. They were always total rubbish. In fact Jazz would buy and sell virtually anything that had or could have had a value and could make him a profit and was always able to talk himself out of trouble when the occasion arose.

He was called Jazz because local rumour had circulated that he had been conceived in the back of a Honda car and his parents thought that the name was in keeping with the circumstances and unique venue of this event.

Jazz had many careers one of them being security guard for J A Hyman and at first he took his responsibilities seriously. After all he was the proud keeper of a high visibility yellow security man's jacket. Alas Jazz being Jazz, the excitement of being the local security man waned very quickly and it seemed to be far more important to be on his mobile phone chatting up the girls or doing some vitally important business deal. The inevitable happened one morning, after a few weeks in the job when he was doing some dodgy deal on his phone and not paying attention to what he should have been when two young local thugs stole a hand bag from one of our customers and he was so engrossed with his wheeling and dealing that he never even noticed.

Relations between him and us became very fractious after that episode and Jazz's career as a security officer was terminated. He did negotiate to keep his yellow high density jacket as a reminder to an illustrious career in security. Something no doubt he would put down on his CV for future employers to ponder over.

After a few months had passed by, relations thawed with our "passed" security man, as it was very difficult to be angry with him for long. He would be seen strutting up and down Waterloo Road, doing deals with the local scallies, making a couple of pounds here and there and posing as king of the Sikhs.

His big moment arrived one fine sunny morning when he was approached by two Italian speaking gentlemen who said that they were looking for directions to Broughton Lane. They had an appointment with one of the locals who had desperately wanted a cam recorder and they had the very latest model which was surplus to their requirement and they were prepared to unload this camera for less than half of the retail price. Jazz, always being the businessman and sensing a bargain and a quick buck, asked to have a look at this new sexy cam recorder in its original box, just the way that it had left the factory. It smelled of newness and profit; it smelled irresistible; it had to be bought.

The Italians told Jazz that they had promised the camera to this gent on Broughton Lane but as Jazz could obviously give it a good home, they would abandon the guy down the road and as long as he kept his mouth shut as to whom he had come across and bought this smart piece of high tech then they would consider Jazz as the lucky owner. All they needed was the modest sum of £250.This caused a problem because although Jazz desperately wanted this camera he had forgotten one tiny, although very important, issue. This being the fact that he was virtually penniless and had only £3.45 on him as well as a 100 rupee note. This was not going to buy the high tech brand new in box piece of kit.

There was only one thing left to do and that was to borrow the money. He asked virtually everyone who worked at JAH but most were already skint by Monday and could not or maybe would not help our intrepid entrepreneur.

A cheque was offered but very quickly refused. There was only one thing left to do as the camera vendors were starting to get a little fractious and becoming jittery. Jazz went straight to Richard, his ex-boss, and after a very eloquent presentation, emerged with the cash. The Italian gentlemen put the camera back in the box and insisted in putting the box in the bag that the camera had been acquired in. Cash counted and given to camera sellers everyone shook hands and the Italians took off smartly down the road in their red Alpha Romeo.

Jazz asked the whole staff for a photo shoot with his new camera and everyone lined up on the forecourt eager to be the first to be photographed by the new artist on the block. Maybe a bit of Hightown history, maybe our very own Indian Lowry. Jazz ceremoniously took the box from the very posh bag and opened the camera box. His face immediately changed from brown to white as he opened the box and a bag of sugar dropped out. He was not amused, although all the staff thought that it was hilarious and they still talk about sugar sweet Jazz The Lad and the vanishing camera.

CHAPTER 35

The Culture Club at Waterloo Road

Shopping can be so boring and mundane. Every week, the same routine. You buy it, cook it, eat it and the next week you start all over again. I thought that my customers deserved a better deal. Why not browse and, whilst doing their retail therapy, spend an hour listening to an interesting speaker on a meaningful and current topic at the same time? To finish, enjoy a cup of tea on us that should brighten anyone's day and stimulate the mind.

This worked for Waterstone's, the bespoke bookshop, so why should it not work for us? After all, my store in Waterloo Road was considered the epicentre of Jewish gastro culture, spanning the complete spectrum of Jewish and kosher life in and around Manchester and the provinces in the North.

Our first speaker was easy to find. An exciting food writer who had just had a book published on Jewish food throughout the world. Perfect for the first venture. This authoress, besides being famous, was my little cousin Clarissa Hyman and besides, she came free.

An advert was to be placed in the Jewish Telegraph, which was published every Friday informing the community that there was to be a culturally interesting speaker who would talk about her new book. This would be a first in a Jewish retail food shop, as the event would be during the day in working hours, in a working shop between the hours of 2 pm until 3.15, so that it would not interfere with the collection of children from school.

I had purposely chosen a Monday afternoon as this was always the quietest retail day and there would not be many customers thronging around the store to interrupt the flow of our very first celebrity speaker. I assumed that all the ladies and maybe the odd gentleman would listen attentively to our Clarissa, ask some pertinent questions, buy her new book, spend some money and tell their friends what a great afternoon that they had had. Maybe some of their acquaintances would come down Waterloo Road to the next exciting event and besides being enthralled by our erudite celebrity, spend some money. But that would be next time and first of all we had to see what would happen on this particular Monday.

The advertisement was placed in the Jewish Telegraph proclaiming that the culture event of the year was to be at the J.A. Hyman store in Waterloo Road on the Monday next, where the very famous Clarissa Hyman would be talking about her new cookery book. Refreshments would be served and the whole event was to be free, except for the books. An enjoyable couple of hours guaranteed for all.

Not having any idea how many people would turn up I had brought from home all surplus folding chairs and stools that were available. About twenty, a few chairs and stools from work, making the figure up to thirty something and hoped that we would fill most of them in the afternoon.

After an uneventful Monday morning, the shop having been made to look more pristine than usual, the chairs and stools were being set out in orderly rows leaving a gap down the middle for swift exits, loo visits and maybe a little shopping.

About 1.30pm people started arriving, sitting themselves down, placing coats on adjoining chairs in order to save for relatives and friends and by 2.00pm an amazing sight, the shop was full and not a spare seat to be had in the house. By the time Clarissa arrived it was standing room only and she was greeted with a generous round of applause. I am not sure who was more surprised, me with the number of people, or her with her very warm welcome.

Clarissa was well into her fascinating talk, relating to us her interesting research in finding out how the recipes had evolved by their various communities and how they had been passed down, mostly orally from mother to daughter and how she had collected many of these recipes from across the world and had put them in a book to ensure that they would be around for posterity. Everyone was sitting or standing and were avidly listening.

Suddenly one of my oldest customers, both in terms of length of time and age, entered the shop and completely ignoring speaker and audience, banged on the counter demanding two ounces of pickled meat and make sure that it is fresh and lean, no fat and an ugurki, a sweet and sour cucumber for her dinner. She then, oblivious to what was going on around her went to the cash register paid for her supper and then walked through the audience and left without a second glance of what was going on around her. The customers, audience and speaker broke into spontaneous applause, thinking that this was one of my jokes and that this lady had been planted to come into the shop by me as a bit of fun in the middle of the action.

Clarissa's talk was a great success, not only did she sell lots of her cookery books, but the audience and customers all went home happy, hopefully to tell all their friends what a good afternoon they had enjoyed. Even the JT and

JG reported that it had been an enlightening occasion. Culture it seemed was spreading up to Waterloo Road. We had found something and if the customer wanted this education on shopping trips we would provide it.

Following on from the successful cookery book talk it was decided to further educate our customers and this time they would be given a more topical talk, something that was in the news and a lot of people were very worried by the scare mongering that had been reported by the Ministry of Agriculture. Something more educational that would make us think; definitely suitable for the intellect and understanding of my customers. This was the alleged mad cow disease. The only time that I had seen mad cows was in the lead up to Pesach, but I digress. This was the disease that could cross between cows and people and kill us all off, so we were told and because of this terrible scare millions of cattle were killed and burnt on huge pyres and the smoke of these huge barbecues could be seen for miles.

A few memorable things came out of this scare. A lot of money was made by the companies that were sold the licences to destroy and burn the cattle. They made a fortune out of the wanton destruction of seemingly healthy cows and bulls. The farmers had been well compensated for their losses so they didn't seem to be too concerned.

With all this going on, it was thought that a good idea for our second talk would be the man from the Livestock Commission who had been asked, and accepted my invitation to speak to the good ladies of Manchester and surrounding areas about mad cow disease. The usual advertising and I felt that this would create a great deal of interest and maybe a lively debate afterwards.

Some forty chairs were put out and at 2.00 pm on the Monday the man from the ministry turned up. Some fifteen minutes later ten ladies arrived. The speaker manfully droned on for nearly an hour. The technical interest in this potentially catastrophic subject was virtually nil. My good ladies in the audience had begun to fidget and, realising what was not happening, I quickly brought the proceedings to a swift close.

That was virtually the end of the culture club for customers. The final throw of the dice was an afternoon with a very nice Sephardi lady who had written a lovely cookery book but by this time all my customers had been cultured out and all they wanted to do was to spend lots of money and just be shoppers.

EPILOGUE

In the words of the Frank Ifield song:

When my life is through
And the angels ask me to recall
The thrill of it all,
then I will tell them
I remember you

THAT'S ALL......... FOR NOW!

Thanks

Stan H

GLOSSARY / STAN SPEAK

Balagan	Chaos
Chazan	Cantor who sings in a synagogue
Chometz	Foods not to be eaten at Passover
Fleishick	Meat
Fress	Eat
Fussnogge	Calves foot jelly
Gaffs	Markets
Gornisht	Nothing
Grob	Uncouth
Kashrut	Kosher
Kvetching	Squeezing
Milchick	Milk
Mitzvah	A good deed
Nash	Snack or treat
Punter	Customer
Schlepping	Carrying
Shadchan	Matchmaker
Shmaltz	Chicken fat
Shmie	Window shopping, browse
Treife	Non-kosher